Of Mice and Men

John Steinbeck

Oxford Literature Companions

Notes and activities: Carmel Waldron
Series consultant: Peter Buckroyd

OXFORD
UNIVERSITY PRESS

Contents

What are Oxford Literature Companions?

Oxford Literature Companions is a series designed to provide you with comprehensive support for popular set texts. You can use the Companion alongside your novel, using relevant sections during your studies or using the book as a whole for revision.

Each Companion includes detailed guidance and practical activities on:

- **Plot and Structure**
- **Context**
- **Characters**
- **Language**
- **Themes**
- **Skills and Practice**

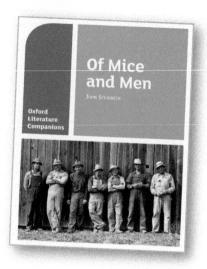

How does this book help with exam preparation?

As well as providing guidance on key areas of the novel, throughout this book you will also find 'Upgrade' features. These are tips to help with your exam preparation and performance.

In addition, in the extensive **Skills and Practice** chapter, the **Exam skills** section provides detailed guidance on areas such as how to prepare for the exam, understanding the question, planning your response and hints for what to do (or not do) in the exam.

In the **Skills and Practice** chapter there is also a bank of **Sample questions** and **Sample answers**. The **Sample answers** are marked and include annotations and a summative comment.

How does this book help with terminology?

Throughout the book, key terms are highlighted in the text and explained on the same page. There is also a detailed **Glossary** at the end of the book that explains, in the context of the novel, all the relevant terms highlighted in this book.

How does this book work?

Each book in the Oxford Literature Companions series follows the same approach and includes the following features:

- **Key quotations** from the novel
- **Key terms** explained on the page and linked to a complete glossary at the end of the book
- **Activity boxes** to help improve your understanding of the text
- **Upgrade** tips to help prepare you for your assessment

To help illustrate the features in this book, here are two annotated pages taken from this Oxford Literature Companion:

Key quotations from the novel

Activity boxes to help improve your understanding of the novel

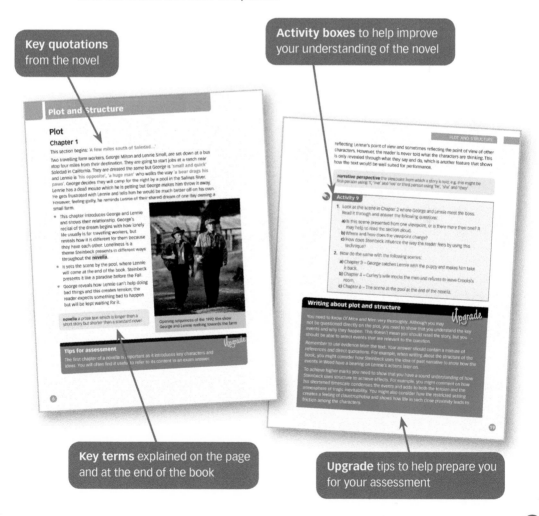

Plot and Structure

Plot
Chapter 1
This section begins: 'A few miles south of Soledad...'

Two travelling farm workers, George Milton and Lennie Small, are set down at a bus stop four miles from their destination. They are going to start jobs at a ranch near Soledad in California. They are dressed the same but George is 'small and quick' and Lennie is 'his opposite', 'a huge man' who walks the way 'a bear drags his paws'. George decides they will camp for the night by a pool in the Salinas River. Lennie has a dead mouse which he is petting but George makes him throw it away. He gets frustrated with Lennie and tells him he would be much better off on his own. However, feeling guilty, he reminds Lennie of their shared dream of one day owning a small farm.

- This chapter introduces George and Lennie and shows their relationship. George's recital of the dream begins with how lonely life usually is for travelling workers, but reveals how it is different for them because they have each other. Loneliness is a theme Steinbeck presents in different ways throughout the **novella**.

- It sets the scene by the pool, where Lennie will come at the end of the book. Steinbeck presents it like a paradise before the Fall.

- George reveals how Lennie can't help doing bad things and this creates tension; the reader expects something bad to happen but will be kept waiting for it.

novella a prose text which is longer than a short story but shorter than a standard novel

Opening sequences of the 1992 film show George and Lennie walking towards the farm

Tips for assessment

The first chapter of a novella is important as it introduces key characters and ideas. You will often find it useful to refer to its content in an exam answer.

Upgrade

PLOT AND STRUCTURE

reflecting Lennie's point of view and sometimes reflecting the point of view of other characters. However, the reader is never told what the characters are thinking. This is only revealed through what they say and do, which is another feature that shows how the text would be well suited for performance.

narrative perspective the viewpoint from which a story is told; e.g. this might be first person using 'I', 'me' and 'we' or third person using 'he', 'she' and 'they'

Activity 9

1. Look at the scene in Chapter 2 where George and Lennie meet the boss. Read it through and answer the following questions:
   a) Is this scene presented from one viewpoint, or is there more than one? It may help to read the section aloud.
   b) Where and how does the viewpoint change?
   c) How does Steinbeck influence the way the reader feels by using this technique?

2. Now do the same with the following scenes:
   a) Chapter 3 – George catches Lennie with the puppy and makes him take it back.
   b) Chapter 4 – Curley's wife mocks the men and refuses to leave Crooks's room.
   c) Chapter 6 – The scene at the pool at the end of the novella.

Writing about plot and structure

Upgrade

You need to know Of Mice and Men very thoroughly. Although you may not be questioned directly on the plot, you need to show that you understand the key events and why they happen. This doesn't mean you should retell the story, but you should be able to select events that are relevant to the question.

Remember to use evidence from the text. Your answer should contain a mixture of references and direct quotations. For example, when writing about the structure of the book, you might consider how Steinbeck uses the idea of past narrative to show how the events in Weed have a bearing on Lennie's actions later on.

To achieve higher marks you need to show that you have a sound understanding of how Steinbeck uses structure to achieve effects. For example, you might comment on how his shortened timescale condenses the events and adds to both the tension and the atmosphere of tragic inevitability. You might also consider how the restricted setting creates a feeling of claustrophobia and shows how life in such close proximity leads to friction among the characters.

Key terms explained on the page and at the end of the book

Upgrade tips to help prepare you for your assessment

Plot

Chapter 1

This section begins: **'A few miles south of Soledad...'**

Two travelling farm workers, George Milton and Lennie Small, are set down at a bus stop four miles from their destination. They are going to start jobs at a ranch near Soledad in California. They are dressed the same but George is **'small and quick'** and Lennie is **'his opposite'**, **'a huge man'** who walks the way **'a bear drags his paws'**. George decides they will camp for the night by a pool in the Salinas River. Lennie has a dead mouse which he is petting but George makes him throw it away. He gets frustrated with Lennie and tells him he would be much better off on his own. However, feeling guilty, he reminds Lennie of their shared dream of one day owning a small farm.

- This chapter introduces George and Lennie and shows their relationship. George's recital of the dream begins with how lonely life usually is for travelling workers, but reveals how it is different for them because they have each other. Loneliness is a theme Steinbeck presents in different ways throughout the **novella**.

- It sets the scene by the pool, where Lennie will come at the end of the book. Steinbeck presents it like a paradise before the Fall.

- George reveals how Lennie can't help doing bad things and this creates tension; the reader expects something bad to happen but will be kept waiting for it.

> **novella** a prose text which is longer than a short story but shorter than a standard novel

Opening sequences of the 1992 film show George and Lennie walking towards the farm

---

Tips for assessment

The first chapter of a novella is important as it introduces key characters and ideas. You will often find it useful to refer to its content in an exam answer.

Activity 1

Look at the opening section of the book from the beginning down to 'the limb is worn smooth by men who have sat on it'.

a) Find three examples of each of the following:

- phrases used to describe the water
- phrases used to describe the surroundings
- phrases used to describe animals
- phrases used to describe people.

b) What kind of atmosphere do these phrases create at the start of the book? Why do you think Steinbeck decided to begin the story in this way? Think about what happens later in the book.

---

jail bait normally a girl under the age of consent; here a woman who could tempt the men into adultery

jerkline skinner the chief driver of a mule train. The mules would pull the carts into which the grain was loaded

Chapter 2

This section begins: 'The bunk house was a long, rectangular building…'

George and Lennie arrive at the ranch. The boss thinks George may be taking advantage of Lennie but George says Lennie is his cousin who was kicked in the head by a horse. The boss hires them and they are shown their bunks by Candy, an elderly cleaner who has 'a round stick-like wrist, but no hand' and has a smelly old dog. Curley the boss's son comes into the bunk house and looks 'coldly at George and then at Lennie'. George tells Lennie to keep away from him. Later Curley's wife enters and George thinks she is **jail bait** but Lennie says, "Gosh, she was purty". Slim, the **jerkline skinner**, on whose team they will be working, introduces himself, as does a big man called Carlson and they talk about Slim's dog who has just had puppies. Carlson says Candy should shoot his old dog because he "Stinks like hell" and get a puppy. George promises Lennie he will ask for a puppy for Lennie to look after.

- Chapter 2 introduces the boss, his son Curley, Curley's wife, Candy and his dog, and Slim and Carlson.
- Steinbeck builds tension as George tells Lennie what to do in case of trouble, using repetition to remind the reader of Lennie's tendency to do bad things.

Activity 2

A number of characters are presented for the first time in this chapter. One such character is Curley's wife.

> **Key quotations**
>
> Both men glanced up, for the rectangle of sunshine in the doorway was cut off. A girl was standing there looking in. She had full, rouged lips and wide-spaced eyes, heavily made up. Her fingernails were red. Her hair hung in little rolled clusters, like sausages. She wore a cotton house dress and red mules, on the insteps of which were little bouquets of red ostrich feathers. "I'm lookin' for Curley," she said. Her voice had a nasal, brittle quality. *(Chapter 2)*

1. Examine this extract carefully and then answer the following questions:

    a) Why does Steinbeck tell us that she blocks out the light?

    b) Why does the author describe her as being **'heavily made up'**?

    c) Her lips, nails and shoes are all red. What do you think Steinbeck wants to show about her by using this colour?

    d) We learn later in the novella that Curley's wife wanted to be an actress. Is this reflected in this first description of her? (You should think about the make-up, the **'bouquets'** of feathers and taking the spotlight.)

    e) What does the phrase **'nasal, brittle quality'** tell us about her voice?

2. Consider the other characters Steinbeck introduces in this chapter – Candy, Curley, Slim and Carlson. Pick out two phrases from each description that reveal something significant about each character. Be prepared to explain your choices.

Chapter 3

This section begins: **'Although there was evening brightness showing...'**

George tells Slim that he's looked after Lennie since his Aunt Clara died. Slim says Lennie is **"a nice fella"** and is impressed by his great strength. George confides that they had to leave Weed, one of the places they worked in previously, because Lennie was accused of rape after he tried to pet a girl's dress.

Carlson offers to shoot Candy's dog painlessly, **"right in the back of the head"**, and Slim agrees with him and offers a puppy to replace it. Carlson takes Candy's dog out and shoots it.

Another ranch hand, Whit, tells George about a brothel the men visit and invites him to go with them. Curley bursts in, looking for his wife, and then rushes out into the

Candy offers to buy into George and Lennie's dream farm

barn after Slim, suspecting that they are together. Whit and Carlson follow, hoping for a fight.

George tells Lennie again about the farm they're saving up for. Old Candy is drawn into the idea too and offers to provide half the money. George calculates that they could have enough money **"Right squack in one month"**.

Curley is confronted by Slim and Carlson, and picks a fight with Lennie, which ends in Curley's hand being crushed.

- Steinbeck uses **foreshadowing** when Carlson shoots Candy's old dog and through reference to Curley's wife as **"jail bait"** *(Chapter 2)*. Lennie's response to Curley's attack, and the injury to Curley's hand, show Lennie's great strength and how he panics. These events anticipate what happens to Lennie and Curley's wife at the end of the book.
- Steinbeck uses irony to show that Candy, one of the weakest characters, can provide the means for the dream to become a reality.
- Steinbeck shows that the dream is within reach, so when it is snatched away, the disappointment is worse.

foreshadowing the use of events in a book that are later shown to have a connection with a more important incident, e.g. the men who chase George and Lennie in Weed foreshadow the men who will hunt Lennie down at the end of the book

9

Activity 3

1. Chapter 3 ends with the fight between Curley and Lennie. Look at how Steinbeck prepares the reader for this climactic moment. You should discuss and make notes on the following:

   - the way Steinbeck introduces Curley in Chapter 2 and George and Lennie's reaction to him
   - Curley's actions and speech when he comes into the bunk house in Chapter 3
   - phrases that show Curley's violence towards Lennie in Chapter 3
   - phrases in Chapter 3 that show Lennie's helplessness and fear.

2. Use your notes to write two or three paragraphs showing the contrast between the ways in which Steinbeck presents Curley and Lennie in this chapter, making reference to his choice of words and phrases.

Chapter 4

This section begins: **'Crooks, the negro stable buck…'**

George and the other ranch hands go into town, leaving only Crooks, Lennie and Candy behind. Lennie invites himself into Crooks's room and the **stable buck** starts to talk about how alone he is because of **segregation** and how important it is **"just bein' with another guy"**. He tries to make Lennie imagine what it would be like if George didn't return, but back-tracks quickly when Lennie becomes threatening.

Lennie tells Crooks about the dream farm but Crooks doesn't believe it will happen because he says he's seen too many travelling workers with the same idea and none of them succeeded in getting their own land.

Later, Candy comes into the harness room and tells Crooks they have enough money to make the dream happen. Crooks sounds more convinced. He tells them if they **"want a hand to work for nothing […] why I'd come an' lend a hand"**. They are interrupted by the arrival of Curley's wife. She demands to know what happened to Curley's hand. Lennie gives himself away because he has bruises on his face and won't look at her directly. Crooks tries to throw her out but she threatens him with **lynching** and when Candy stands up to her, she just tells him, **"Nobody'd listen to you"**. She finally leaves when Candy says the other men are coming back.

- This chapter brings out the themes of loneliness and racism.
- The reader learns more about Curley's wife – her nasty side, but also her isolation. She is shown abusing the weakest members of the ranch, but her admiration of Lennie's strength also foreshadows the fatal attention she pays him later on.
- Steinbeck reveals the hierarchy at the ranch through the way the characters interact with one another. For example, the conversation between Crooks and Lennie reveals Lennie's vulnerability without George.

lynching the illegal hanging of someone (usually from a tree) by a group or mob without a proper arrest or trial

segregation the separation of white people and black people in many areas of life, such as: accommodation, transport, education and public facilities

stable buck a racist term for a black stable lad or groom

Activity 4

1. This chapter shows the 'misfits' on the ranch together. Steinbeck shows us that even among these characters there is a kind of hierarchy. Re-read the chapter and discuss the following questions:

   a) Who do you think has the most power in this chapter? What makes you think this? Write down two or three phrases from the text to support your view.

   b) Who has the least power, in your opinion? Justify your answer with reference to the text.

   c) Steinbeck tells us that Crooks **'was a proud, aloof man'**. What impression does this give you of him? Does the rest of the chapter strengthen this view or does it make you want to change your opinion? Select two or three phrases from the text to help you explain your views.

Chapter 5

This section begins: 'One end of the great barn was piled high…'

Having accidentally killed his puppy, Lennie shouts at it: "God damn you" [...] "Why do you got to get killed? You ain't so little as mice." He is angry but also guilty and afraid.

Curley's wife seems fascinated by Lennie. She tells him how she could have been an actress or a film star, although it is obvious to

Lennie strokes Curley's wife's hair

the reader that she has been strung along by empty compliments from men: "He says he was gonna put me in the movies. Says I was a natural."

She asks about Lennie's love of petting things and invites him to stroke her hair. When he strokes it harder, she gets angry. He tries to stop her yelling and breaks her neck. Lennie realizes the severity of his actions: 'he whispered in fright, "I done a bad thing. I done another bad thing".' Then he remembers what George told him and heads for the pool of the river.

Candy finds Curley's wife's body and calls George. He begs George to buy the farm anyway but knows it is hopeless. He gets angry, shouting at her body, **"Ever'body knowed you'd mess things up."** George tries to believe that Lennie will be captured and treated as mentally ill, but Slim tells him, **"Curley's gonna want to shoot 'im."** Then Curley, who is suspicious of George, and Carlson set off with guns to shoot Lennie.

- The dead puppy foreshadows the death of Curley's wife – too much petting and then panic. As soon as she lets Lennie stroke her hair, the reader knows what will happen. The author creates a sense of **inevitability** about the murder and Lennie's reaction to it.

- Steinbeck shows George's affection for Lennie in his desperate hope that Lennie will be treated fairly – a hope dashed by Slim.

- Steinbeck presents Slim as George's **accomplice** and sympathizer.

> **accomplice** a person who helps another to commit a crime
>
> **inevitability** the way in which something becomes absolutely certain because of the circumstances leading up to it

Activity 5

Discuss and make notes on the following questions:

a) Why does Lennie talk with Curley's wife after George has told him not to?
b) Why does George let Candy know the dream farm cannot happen?
c) Why does Candy blame Curley's wife after she is dead?
d) Why does Curley insist George goes with them after Lennie?

Chapter 6

This section begins: **'The deep green pool of the Salinas River…'**

This begins in a similar way to the first chapter with the description of the pool and Lennie sitting on his own. When George finds him, the reader is not sure what will happen. Lennie cries to him: **"You ain't gonna leave me, are ya, George?"** When George repeats his 'giving hell' speech and then the dream, it is a reminder of the first chapter when these things were still possible. Now the reader knows they are not.

When George brings out the gun it is clear what he is going to do and that he is going to do it out of love.

George soothes Lennie so he doesn't realize what is happening and tells him: "I never been mad, an' I ain't now. That's a thing I want ya to know." He shoots Lennie in the same way Carlson shoots the old dog.

Curly and Carlson believe Lennie took the gun and George shot him in self-defence, but Slim knows better. He takes George for a drink, saying, "You hadda, George. I swear you hadda." Ironically, George is now free from the burden of having to look after Lennie, but nobody will imagine he is happy about it. The end of Lennie is also the end of the dream because it included him.

George comforts Lennie and tells him he will not leave him

- The story comes full circle, but the paradise is now overshadowed by death.

- Steinbeck shows that Lennie has a conscience but he is mainly worried about being abandoned by George. The author is making it clear that he would never survive the fate Curley has planned for him.

- The repetition of the dream story is now sadly **ironic**, in contrast with the first chapter, but Steinbeck uses it for George to represent a kind of heaven that Lennie will now inhabit after he dies.

- Curley and Carlson have little **empathy** with George, and Steinbeck uses their views to represent the majority opinion in this society. Only Slim knows what Lennie meant to George and has the intelligence to realize George's dilemma.

empathy understanding of another person's feelings

ironic the way in which something is shown to be the opposite of what is said

Activity 6

You are going to set up a trial for George where he will be tried for the murder of Lennie. Your aim is to arrive at a verdict of guilty or not guilty.

Work in groups of seven. You should appoint a judge, a prosecution counsel, a defence counsel and some witnesses. The two counsels should write their questions and speeches based on events in the book.

Use the information in the panels below and at the top of page 15 to help you set up the trial. Practise the trial before presenting it to the class.

Prosecution counsel

The prosecution counsel is trying to get a verdict of 'guilty' against George for the murder of Lennie. The counsel will want to put questions to the witnesses that show George intended to kill Lennie and murdered him in cold blood. The counsel will also want to show that George was depriving Lennie of a fair trial, so will play down any suggestion of a lynch mob. Questions will encourage Curley and Carlson to say they only wanted to capture Lennie and hand him over to the law (supported by Whit being sent for the deputy sheriff). The prosecution counsel will try to discredit the defence witnesses and show that they are lying if possible. Quoting the witnesses' words can be a useful way to do this.

Defence counsel

The defence counsel is trying to get a verdict of 'not guilty' for George. The counsel will want to put questions to the witnesses that show George acted in self-defence and that he found Lennie just ahead of the search party, which was actually a lynch mob. Questions will encourage Candy and Slim to repeat Curley's threats against Lennie and show why George might have wanted to find Lennie first. The defence counsel will try to discredit prosecution witnesses and show that they are lying if possible. Making direct reference to the witnesses' words is a good way to do this.

George

The person playing George should study his behaviour in the novella and write a speech in his defence. George cannot tell the real truth about his motives for shooting Lennie because this would not be a legal defence. He can admit to shooting Lennie, while trying to leave the exact circumstances unclear as far as possible to avoid perjury (lying under oath). Try to use George's own words wherever possible.

Prosecution witnesses

Prosecution witnesses might include Curley and Carlson, who should work together on their version of events, based on Chapters 5 and 6, sticking to the story that they only wanted to hand Lennie to the law for trial. Try to use these characters' own words wherever possible.

Defence witnesses

Defence witnesses might include Slim and Candy. Candy can testify to Curley's threats against Lennie and his refusal to stay with his dead wife. Slim can testify to what he saw when he arrived at the pool, but without saying what he knows must have happened. Try to use these characters' own words wherever possible.

The judge

The judge should decide on the verdict based on the evidence presented.

Structure

The novella is structured according to a classic plotline. The **protagonists** – George and Lennie – have a goal which they try to achieve; in this case getting their own farm. Outside forces obstruct their way to the goal; here these forces are Lennie's talent for trouble as well as Curley and his wife.

There are two possible outcomes to this type of plotline. Either the protagonists overcome the obstacles and achieve their goal (at one point this seems possible with Candy's help) or they fail – and this is what actually happens in *Of Mice and Men*.

protagonists the central characters

Timescale and setting

Of Mice and Men is unusual in that Steinbeck intended it to be a play as well as a prose narrative. This is reflected in the way the events of the plot take place over the course of a single weekend, opening with sunset on Thursday evening and closing with the sunset on Sunday evening; the dying of the day providing a suitable backdrop for Lennie's death.

The novella has only three settings – the pool by the Salinas River, the bunk house and the barn (which includes Crooks's quarters). It is written mostly in dialogue with a limited cast of characters. Each chapter also represents a separate 'scene'.

1. The pool on Thursday evening.

2. The bunk house on Friday morning.

3. The bunk house on Friday evening.

4. The barn/harness room on Saturday evening.

5. The barn on Sunday afternoon.

6. The pool on Sunday evening.

The plot moves from an opening which hints at the possibility of disaster, through to the unfolding of the dream (which almost becomes a reality) to the inevitable destruction of both Lennie and the dream.

Activity 7

1. Complete the following tasks:

   a) Discuss and make notes about why you think Steinbeck chose to set his story over the course of a single weekend. What are the effects of using such a tight timescale? Does this affect the way the reader sees the characters? Is there enough time to get to know them?

   b) What is your opinion about the very limited locations in the book? How are they contrasted? What effect does this have on mood and atmosphere in the novella?

2. Write two or three paragraphs explaining the effects of Steinbeck's decision to restrict the timescale and setting in this way.

Foreshadowing

The plot moves in a circle, opening and closing with the pool, the heron, the water snake and George and Lennie sitting on the bank. In between, there are a series of events that make the hopes of the opening impossible. George's advice to Lennie to hide if he gets into trouble sows the seeds for tragedy and these come to fruition when Lennie realizes that he has killed Curley's wife.

Throughout the book Steinbeck builds up a series of incidents that create a sense of **foreboding** and anticipate the final, tragic outcome.

George knows that Lennie will find peace and refuge at the pool

- In the opening chapter Steinbeck shows how Lennie's love of petting soft things gets him and George into trouble.

- Curley's aggression leads George to warn Lennie to keep away from Curley and he repeats his instructions about what to do if Lennie gets into trouble.
- Curley's wife appears in the bunk house and Lennie admires her. George senses trouble and tells him to have nothing to do with her.
- The shooting of Candy's old dog shows the men's attitude to any animal (or person) that is unable to look after itself.
- The frequent appearances of Curley looking for his wife or Curley's wife allegedly seeking her husband create tension because we know they both mean trouble.
- The scene in Crooks's room shows how much power Curley's wife has when she decides to use it. Her admiration of Lennie for taking on Curley also creates suspense as we know what George and others have said about her.
- The sense of foreboding increases as Steinbeck shows Lennie sitting in the barn with the dead puppy and the tension rises with the entrance of Curley's wife and with references to the men just outside the barn who might come in at any moment.

> **foreboding** a prediction or omen that suggests something bad is going to happen

Cause and effect

When thinking about the structure of a novel, you might look at **cause and effect**. This is the way in which one action leads to another and how this works to create the plot. Steinbeck uses this technique to build up expectations in the reader. For example, when we have been told that Slim is the main authority on the ranch and he refuses to intercede for Candy's dog, we know there is no hope for the animal and, by extension, not much hope for Candy either.

Steinbeck also uses cause and effect to create tension in the story. This is the case when we are shown Lennie's first encounter with Curley. Later, having just been humiliated by Slim and Carlson, Curley sees Lennie smiling. The reader knows Curley will pick on Lennie, but Steinbeck creates tension as the reader has to wait to find out how Lennie will react

> **cause and effect** the way in which one event leads to or creates another event

Cause and effect is what creates a plot rather than just a story. In most novels, the plot will usually have a three-part structure:

1. the set-up
2. the conflict
3. the climax and resolution.

Activity 8

Create a visual layout of the three-part structure in *Of Mice and Men*, either on paper or on screen as a digital presentation. Add comments and pictures to your design to highlight key events and to show why they are important in the novella.

Your layout should show the following:

Part 1. The set-up

This will be the shortest section in which the protagonists are introduced and the **inciting incident** occurs. This is the event that triggers everything that happens later on. What do you think the inciting incident is in *Of Mice and Men*? Is it the incident in Weed that happens before the story begins? Or is it the fact that George and Lennie get work on a ranch that includes Curley and his wife?

Part 2. The conflict

This will be the longest section and will include key events leading up to the climax of the plot. You could present this as a linked chain showing causes and effects. Which events do you think should be included here? How do these events link together?

Part 3. The climax and resolution

This will be a fairly short section. It will include the **climax** – a major event that everything has been leading towards – and a **resolution** – how everything is worked out. What is the climax in *Of Mice and Men*? What is the resolution? How does this resolution make you feel as a reader?

Remember to include page references and quotations that will help you with your revision.

climax a turning point in the action of a novel; the moment where the action reaches its greatest intensity

inciting incident an important event in the plot that triggers everything that happens later on

resolution how the climax or crisis in a narrative is worked out

Perspective

Steinbeck wrote *Of Mice and Men* so that it could easily be adapted into a play. This is partly reflected in Steinbeck's choice of the **narrative perspective**, which is third person, allowing him to shift the focus from one character to another. Steinbeck also adapts the viewpoint, sometimes reflecting George's point of view, sometimes reflecting Lennie's point of view and sometimes reflecting the point of view of other characters. However, the reader is never told what the characters are thinking. This is only revealed through what they say and do, which is another feature that shows how the text would be well suited for performance.

> **narrative perspective** the viewpoint from which a story is told; e.g. this might be first person using 'I', 'me' and 'we' or third person using 'he', 'she' and 'they'

Activity 9

1. Look at the scene in Chapter 2 where George and Lennie meet the boss. Read it through and answer the following questions:

   a) Is this scene presented from one viewpoint, or is there more than one? It may help to read the section aloud.
   b) Where and how does the viewpoint change?
   c) How does Steinbeck influence the way the reader feels by using this technique?

2. Now do the same with the following scenes:

   a) Chapter 3 – George catches Lennie with the puppy and makes him take it back.
   b) Chapter 4 – Curley's wife mocks the men and refuses to leave Crooks's room.
   c) Chapter 6 – The scene at the pool at the end of the novella.

Writing about plot and structure

Upgrade

You need to know *Of Mice and Men* very thoroughly. Although you may not be questioned directly on the plot, you need to show that you understand the key events and why they happen. This doesn't mean you should retell the story, but you should be able to select events that are relevant to the question.

Remember to use evidence from the text. Your answer should contain a mixture of references and direct quotations. For example, when writing about the structure of the book, you might consider how Steinbeck uses the idea of past narrative to show how the events in Weed have a bearing on Lennie's actions later on.

To achieve higher marks you need to show that you have a sound understanding of how Steinbeck uses structure to achieve effects. For example, you might comment on how his shortened timescale condenses the events and adds to both the tension and the atmosphere of tragic inevitability. You might also consider how the restricted setting creates a feeling of claustrophobia and shows how life in such close proximity leads to friction among the characters.

Biography of John Steinbeck

- John Steinbeck was born in 1902 in Salinas, California, the setting for *Of Mice and Men*. He knew the area well, which enabled him to provide authentic descriptive details.

- Steinbeck worked as a **bindle stiff** for a while, like George and Lennie, which means he was familiar with their way of life, their speech and the way they acted. His personal experiences would also have helped him to develop sympathy for the hardship and poverty that many people faced.

- Steinbeck dropped out of Stanford University and became a construction worker and then a reporter, before publishing novels. Being a reporter must have helped him to see things as a journalist would, with a view to a dramatic headline or a human interest story. Reporting would also have influenced his economical style of writing, since news stories have to be concise and to the point.

John Steinbeck (1902–1968)

- Steinbeck married Carol Henning in 1930 and she helped him achieve his first success as a novelist in 1935 with *Tortilla Flat*. *Of Mice and Men* was published in 1937. He divorced Carol in 1941.

- He wrote many more novels including *The Grapes of Wrath* in 1940 for which he was later awarded the Pulitzer Prize for Literature. In 1962 he was awarded the Nobel Prize for Literature.

- During the Second World War Steinbeck worked as a foreign correspondent. He died in 1968 in New York City.

- His novels are notable for their social concerns, especially the effect of the **Great Depression** on working people.

> **bindle stiff** a manual labourer who travelled from place to place to find work
>
> **Great Depression** a period of severe economic depression which affected people across the world in the 1930s

Tips for assessment

In your assessment, you should only mention the author's background in relation to how it may have influenced the text and where this is relevant to the question.

Historical and cultural context of the novella

The 'American Dream'

Of Mice and Men deals with the ideal of the 'American Dream' – the idea that anyone with sufficient motivation and hard work can achieve what they want. As Steinbeck said: 'Socialism never took root in America because the poor see themselves not as an exploited **proletariat** but as temporarily embarrassed millionaires.'

Of course wealth and personal success remain a dream for all the characters in the book as none of them have the economic power or social freedom to realize it.

The Great Depression

The Great Depression was a period of severe economic hardship for people across the world. It was triggered by the **Wall Street Crash** of 1929, which was caused by the value of shares on the **stock market** collapsing and banks going out of business. This meant that many people lost all their savings and the money they had borrowed suddenly had to be repaid, which most people were unable to do. The situation was made worse for American farmers by a succession of severe droughts. In the Midwest these conditions, combined with extensive farming and little protection from wind erosion, effectively turned the soil to dust.

> **proletariat** the common or working people
>
> **stock market** a virtual market in which company shares are traded across the world
>
> **Wall Street Crash** a devastating stock market crash in 1929 which signalled the beginning of the Great Depression

Drought and dust storms ruined farmland across the Midwest in the 1930s

The midwest 'Dust Bowl' ruined millions of acres of land and resulted in disastrous harvests. Many farm workers travelled to California, which had a longer growing season and a wider range of crops. However, these workers were dependent on the landowners and employers who had the power to give them work. The sheer number of people looking for work at the same time kept wages low.

Like migrant fruit-pickers in the UK nowadays, George and Lennie are typical of the travelling workers who had to go where the crops needed harvesting. If the barley was ripe they were needed for that, if a fruit crop was ready they would help with that and they had to keep travelling to find this seasonal work. At a time when the unemployment rate was 25% workers were lucky to find jobs at all. Often they were placed with employers through **work agencies**, like 'Murray and Ready' *(Chapter 2)*, which would provide work cards and bus fares, but also take a cut of the men's wages to pay for their services.

> **public relief** government aid for the poor
>
> **work agencies** places that matched workers to employers, similar to our job centres. They would advance fares to the workers they placed and would then claim these, and their commission, back from their wages

1.3 million farm workers trekked to California in the 1930s hoping for a better life

Although systems of **public relief** were set up to help the unemployed, they were limited and many people preferred not to use them. Candy is fearful of being cast "on the county" *(Chapter 3)* in his old age. Living conditions among the migrant workers' families were often extremely poor. This is why many men travelled to look for seasonal work to try to improve their families' standard of living.

Activity 1

You have been asked to contribute a five-minute slot for a radio programme about the Great Depression in California. Your contribution is about how Steinbeck presented the effects of this in *Of Mice and Men*. Work with a partner and write the script for your slot. You should include:

- how Steinbeck's own experience as a 'bindle stiff' helped him to create a vivid impression of migrant workers in the novella

- how Steinbeck shows that George and Lennie are poor (e.g. their clothes, their food, their desperation for work and their anxiety not to get **'canned'**)

- how Steinbeck reveals the rootless nature of the men's lives (e.g. think about the men who are mentioned but do not appear and the role of the minor characters)

- how Steinbeck reveals the captivating effect of the American Dream, while also making it clear how impossible the dream actually is.

You should use quotations from the text to support your ideas. You could also find a suitable piece of music to play at the beginning and end of your slot. Record your radio presentation to play to the class.

Life in California

California's geographical features include mountains like the Sierra Nevada and deserts like the Mojave as well as the Pacific coastline and fertile valleys. The population erupted with the Gold Rush just prior to 1850 and the area grew prosperous through gold mining and agriculture.

With the coming of the Great Depression, California proved a magnet to outsiders. Many men left their families in order to travel to find work. They were often lonely because they rarely stayed anywhere long enough to make friends. They worked long hours for little pay and, instead of saving or sending their money home, many men were likely to spend it on drinking, gambling and brothels.

Key quotations

"An' where's George now? In town in a whore house. That's where your money's goin'. Jesus, I seen it happen too many times. I seen too many guys with land in their head. They never get none under their hand." *(Crooks, Chapter 4)*

Prejudice and discrimination

Crooks

There was much discrimination in America before the 1960s. Although there were few black Americans in California, which had never been a slave-owning state, the same discrimination seems to have operated there as in the southern states, thanks to the **Jim Crow laws**. This is shown in the scene where Curley's wife threatens Crooks with lynching. This is not an idle threat because, at that time in America, a white woman's complaint against a black man would have been quite enough to get him hanged.

Curley's wife

Curley's wife is herself the victim of discrimination. For example, Steinbeck deliberately presents her as 'Curley's wife' only and the reader never learns her first name. She is shown only as a possession of Curley's or as a likely cause of trouble for the other men. Her dream of being in the "pitchers" (Chapter 4) is one that many girls probably had at the time; it had been the storyline of more than one Hollywood film and Hollywood itself was making money, even through the Great Depression. Films like *42nd Street*, for example, told the story of a talented woman's route to stardom and offered escape from the harsh realities of everyday life.

Clara Bow was a famous actress in the 1930s and many women would have envied her glamorous life

Candy and Lennie

Candy and Lennie are also victims of prejudice. Candy is the victim of prejudice against anyone too old or ill to do their fair share of work. Lennie, disabled by his mental problems, is given little understanding by society, which would sooner imprison him in a jail or a mental institution than treat him according to his needs.

Activity 4

What do we learn about prejudice from:

- the men's attitude to Curley's wife in Chapter 2
- the way Candy and the dog are treated in Chapter 3
- Lennie's visit to Crooks in Chapter 4?

Modern attitudes

The book was written and set in the 1930s and ways of thinking and attitudes have changed considerably since then. Racism and sexism are no longer acceptable – and in fact are illegal. Modern readers will be uncomfortable with the use of the word 'nigger' which is used in the book; if you have to use it in your answer, you should always put it in quotation marks. Modern readers will also feel unhappy about the way Curley's wife is treated and spoken about. The **African-American Civil Rights Movement** had not yet started nor had the **Women's Liberation Movement**. There was no automatic state provision of care for the unemployed, the sick or the elderly and there was little understanding of the educational or welfare needs of the mentally impaired. All of these things need to be taken into account when reading and writing about the book.

African-American Civil Rights Movement a political movement in the USA (1955–1968) aimed at outlawing racial discrimination and giving voting and other rights to black citizens

Jim Crow laws a system of racial segregation laws enacted in the USA between 1876 and 1965

Women's Liberation Movement a broadly based political movement (1965–present) dedicated to giving women equal rights with men under the law, in the workplace and in society

Segregation in the 1930s officially meant 'separate, but equal'; too often it meant inferior or worse

Title of the book

The title *Of Mice and Men* comes from a poem by the famous Scottish poet Robert Burns (1759–96), called 'To a Mouse'. In the poem Burns writes about a field mouse whose carefully built home is destroyed by a plough.

The lines from which the title comes are: 'the best laid plans of mice and men gang oft agley/And leave us naught but grief and pain for promised joy'. This means that however well we plan things they often go wrong and instead of the happiness we imagined we are left with sorrow and disappointment. Burns himself was a farmer and the poem connects us with the setting of the novella and with Lennie's petting of mice, as well as the main theme of shattered dreams.

The final lines of the poem are shown below.

> Still, thou art blest, compar'd wi' me!
> The present only toucheth thee:
> But Och! I backward cast my e'e,
> On prospects drear!
> An forward, tho' I canna see,
> I guess an' fear!

These lines mean that the mouse is better off because it lives in the present, while the writer, Burns, can only see misery when he looks back and, although he cannot see the future, he can guess it and he fears it will be even worse. This reflects the situations in the novella well and ties in with Steinbeck's use of foreshadowing as a technique.

Harvest mice build their intricate nests precariously perched among corn stalks – all too easily destroyed

Activity 5

1. Do you think that 'Of Mice and Men' is an effective title for the book? Explain your ideas.

2. How else might the **juxtaposition** of 'mice' and 'men' be relevant to the novella as a whole?

juxtaposition to place two images or ideas side-by-side to highlight the differences between them

Activity 6

1. Carry out an online search to find out what life was like for migrant workers in California in the 1930s from photographs and people's comments. Find quotations from the novella that link to your research.

2. Use another search to find out what kind of work farmers and ranch hands were doing in the Salinas valley in the 1930s. Try to find photographs and accounts from people. Support your findings with quotations from the novella.

3. Make a wall display using your research, adding quotations and your own explanations.

Writing about context

Upgrade

You may need to relate *Of Mice and Men* to its social, cultural and historical context. To gain marks for this area you need to use your knowledge of the background and setting of the novella to help you answer the question. This does not mean you should write everything you know about it! You need to show how knowing something about the time and place in which the novella is set helps to reveal meaning and shed light on Steinbeck's intentions.

For example, if you are asked a question about (or involving) Curley's wife, it would be difficult to answer it fully without mentioning that her actions reflect the worst side of racial prejudice shown at the time. You might also show some awareness of how the American film industry had provided a new kind of dream of becoming a star. It would also be appropriate to link her position on the ranch with your knowledge of how opportunities for women were limited at this time and how women were expected to become housewives and confine themselves to domestic duties.

As modern readers we have the benefit of hindsight and so the way we read the book is different to how people may have read Steinbeck's novella at the time it was published. Although racism and sexism continue to be a part of some people's thinking, they are no longer condoned by any public body and there are laws prohibiting anyone from inciting racial hatred or discriminating against people on grounds of race or gender. That makes it more difficult for us to understand the attitudes of people in the novella, although it helps to make Lennie, who doesn't discriminate, a more sympathetic character.

Main characters

George Milton

> **Key quotations**
>
> The first man was small and quick, dark of face, with restless eyes and sharp, strong features. Every part of him was defined: small, strong hands, slender arms, a thin and bony nose. *(Chapter 1)*

Sharpness is what characterizes George – both of body and mind. He is quick thinking, as he needs to be to get himself and Lennie out of trouble all the time. We can see this in the second chapter when the boss asks him why they left Weed and he replies that the job was finished. He thinks on his feet and explains that they were digging a cesspit, which would take a relatively short amount of time to complete.

George is 'one of the boys' in that he joins in with the games of cards and horseshoes with the other ranch workers and goes into town with them. He remains different from them, however, in that he has Lennie to look after. This is shown in the opening chapter: **"Lennie, for God' sakes don't drink so much"** [...] **"You gonna be sick like you was last night"** *(Chapter 1)*. His words reveal his protective attitude towards his companion.

George also gets frustrated with Lennie, especially when Lennie doesn't understand or remember things. Lennie's demand for ketchup with his beans, for example, drives George to lose his temper: **"God a'mighty, if I was alone I could live so easy. I could go get a job an' work, an' no trouble. No mess at all, and when the end of the month come I could take my fifty bucks and go into town and get whatever I want"** *(Chapter 1)*. His outburst doesn't last long, however, and he is soon ashamed of it when he sees how frightened Lennie is. George is almost like an older brother or a parent; he sometimes gets annoyed but he knows the other man is dependent on him.

Activity 1

1. Create a pen portrait of George. A pen portrait is like a picture or photograph but in writing. It does more than show what someone looks like – it shows their character as well.

   a) Start by making a list of his character traits (e.g. quick-witted, compassionate, one of the lads, dreamer, etc.). For each character trait you identify, find at least one example from the text that reveals this trait.

   b) Next, use the list of traits and the examples you have found to build a description of George's character. Present your pen portrait either as a piece of writing, as a mini-presentation, or as a wall display. Make sure you include detailed references and quotations to support your ideas.

   c) Discuss what stands out most about George's character. What impact does this have on the novella as a whole?

George is, in his own way, a storyteller. When Lennie begs him to tell him about the future they have planned, he agrees, much like a parent reading a bedtime story: 'George's voice became deeper. He repeated his words rhythmically as though he had said them many times before' *(Chapter 1)*.

Aside from Lennie, George doesn't trust many people. When he finds a can of lice powder by his bunk, he takes some convincing that the mattress is clean. He is also suspicious of Candy when the old man wants to share the future **smallholding**. He takes an instant dislike to Curley and seems to know instinctively that "mean little guys" *(Chapter 2)* like him mean trouble. He tells Lennie to stay away from him and also to keep away from Curley's wife: " 'cause she's a rattrap if ever I seen one" *(Chapter 2)*.

> **smallholding** a property smaller than a normal farm

George is aware that the life he lives is a hard one and there is no place for women. He treats Curley's wife with wary contempt, as do the other ranch hands, seeing her as "a tart" *(Chapter 2)*. He sees visiting a brothel as the way to satisfy his sexual needs without complications, which means that his view of women (like most of the other men on the ranch) is to see them as sexual objects.

George needs Lennie as a companion and as someone to work for. When their dream future actually seems possible, thanks to Candy's money, he imagines the three of them living together. When Lennie kills Curley's wife, his dream is shattered too: "I should of knew," George said hopelessly. "I guess maybe way back in my head I did" *(Chapter 5)*.

Activity 2

Look at the conversation between George and Slim, from '"It wasn't nothing," said Slim…' to '"and he'll do any damn thing, I –"' in Chapter 3.

Discuss the following questions:

- How has the relationship between George and Lennie changed over time?
- What are the reasons for this change?
- What confession does George make to Slim?
- What do you think George's feelings are towards Lennie at this point in the book?

Make brief notes and select useful quotations to keep for your revision.

We realize the extent of George's love for Lennie when he shoots him rather than condemning him to a violent death or life in a brutal institution. It is a dreadful moral decision for George and at first he tries to convince himself that society will treat Lennie decently: 'George stepped close. "Couldn' we maybe bring him in an' they'll lock him up? He's nuts, Slim. He never done this to be mean" *(Chapter 5)*. However, George knows deep down that this won't happen. His action is the

George cares so much that he's prepared to shoot Lennie rather than let him get caught

ultimate act of compassion. He tells Lennie the story he loves about the farm and the rabbits and then kills him instantly; killing his own hopes and dreams in the process.

George's main function in the story is to fulfil the role of Lennie's companion and carer. Steinbeck highlights the contrast between his sharpness and Lennie's slowness; his small build and Lennie's large size. Steinbeck also uses the characterization of George to reveal that in spite of George's intelligence and ability, he is unlikely to achieve a happy future without Lennie to share his plans.

Activity 3

Steinbeck reveals George's care for Lennie in different ways throughout the novella.

1. Make notes on how it is revealed:

   a) in the first chapter of the book

   b) before and after the fight with Curley

   c) at the end of the book.

2. Discuss and make notes on George's use of playing cards in the text. You should consider:

   a) what is special about the game of Solitaire (Patience)

   b) how cards are connected with games of chance.

3. Using your notes from Questions 1 and 2, write a response to the following questions. Does George's attitude towards Lennie change over the course of the story or does it stay the same? What effect does this have on the way you view George in the novella?

Lennie Small

...a huge man, shapeless of face, with large, pale eyes, with wide sloping shoulders [...] he walked heavily, dragging his feet a little, the way a bear drags his paws. His arms did not swing at his sides, but hung loosely. *(Chapter 1)*

Steinbeck's first description of Lennie makes use of animal imagery – he is shown drinking from the pool 'snorting into the water like a horse' *(Chapter 1)*. The images are reinforced again with 'Lennie dabbled his big paw in the water' *(Chapter 1)*. We are not told outright that Lennie has mental difficulties but these comparisons, combined with George's way of speaking to him, give us this impression. Lennie imitates George's actions, which indicates that he looks up to him. He also seems aware of his limitations as he tells George: "I forgot" [...] "I tried not to forget. Honest to God I did, George" *(Chapter 1)*.

The next thing we find out about Lennie is that he loves to pet soft things. Unfortunately, he doesn't realize his own strength and has a tendency to pet things too hard and kill them. In his pocket he has a dead mouse. He tells George: "I could pet it with my thumb while we walked along" *(Chapter 1)*. He gets little sympathy from George who had to get them both out of trouble in Weed because of Lennie's desire to pet a woman's dress. He explains to George the problem with petting mice: "They was so little" [...] "I'd pet 'em, and pretty soon they bit

my fingers and I pinched their heads a little and then they was dead – because they was so little" *(Chapter 1)*. Lennie thinks that the problem is the small size of the mice, rather than the fact that he is too rough, which is another symptom of his childlike outlook. George says he will get Lennie a puppy because he might not kill it, which is ironic in view of what happens later in the story.

Lennie's love of petting things has got him into trouble before and the reader knows it will do so again

Lennie loves to hear the story of the farm he and George will have in the future, mainly because he will be allowed to tend (and presumably pet) the rabbits. He knows the story off by heart but he still likes George to tell it. He breaks in occasionally to add in the things he remembers: 'Lennie broke in. *"But not us! An' why? Because... because I got you to look after me, and you got me to look after you, and that's why."* He laughed delightedly' *(Chapter 1)*. This reinforces his childlike innocence, as does his threat to go off by himself if George doesn't want him, reflecting a child's threat to run away from home.

Activity 4

How do the following incidents reveal Lennie's reliance on George:

- the throwing away of the mouse in Chapter 1
- the interview with the boss in Chapter 2
- the fight with Curley in Chapter 3
- the teasing of Crooks in Chapter 4?

Lennie's great strength is a source of pride. Slim comments: "I never seen such a worker." [...] "God awmighty I never seen such a strong guy" *(Chapter 3)*. However, the same strength is also a source of danger. This is shown when Curley picks a fight with him. Lennie does not fight back until George tells him to, but the result is that Curley's hand gets crushed.

Lennie also shows a childish lack of self-control and impatience. We see this when Crooks suggests that George could leave him: 'Suddenly Lennie's eyes centred and grew quiet, and mad. He stood up and walked dangerously toward Crooks.' *(Chapter 4)*. His anger towards the dead puppy is another example. He shouts at it for getting itself killed before hurling it away from him.

Lennie tends to panic when people shout at him. His panic makes him hang on to them and try to make them stop, which generally leads to disaster. This is why Curley ends up with a crushed hand and his wife with a broken neck. In the first instance George has to take violent action to bring Lennie to his senses and make him let go, but George is not around when Curley's wife invites Lennie to pet her hair.

Tips for assessment

Upgrade

Exam questions may ask you to write about the role or function of a character or perhaps how Steinbeck has chosen to present this character in the text. Remember to focus on whichever aspect you have been asked about.

Activity 5

Look at the conversation between Crooks and Lennie in Chapter 4 that begins **'His voice grew soft and persuasive...'** and finishes **"Maybe I better go see"**.

1. Make a chart to show how Lennie's responses change throughout this passage, marking the different points with quotations. The outline below shows how you might present this. For example: you could plot more aggressive behaviour closer to the top of the chart and calmer behaviour closer to the bottom of the chart.

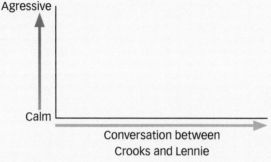

2. Look at the quotation below and discuss what this behaviour reveals about Lennie. Is he responding to Crooks's reference to the **"booby hatch"** (mental asylum) (Chapter 4) or is there another reason for his anger? Why does Steinbeck show this side of Lennie's character at this point in the story?

Key quotations

Suddenly Lennie's eyes centred and grew quiet, and mad. He stood up and walked dangerously toward Crooks. "Who hurt George?" he demanded. *(Chapter 4)*

Lennie does have a conscience and he knows when he's done "a bad thing" *(Chapter 5)*. When he hides in the brush beside the pool at the end of the book, it takes the form first of his Aunt Clara, telling him how useless he is and then takes the shape of a giant rabbit which says: **"You ain't fit to lick the boots of no rabbit. You'd forget 'em and let 'em go hungry. That's what you'd do"** *(Chapter 6)*.

The one thing that makes Lennie frantic with fear is the thought of George leaving him and it is this knowledge that helps George to make his difficult decision. Lennie dies happy as George tells him the familiar story he loves and because of George's actions he is spared the terror of lynching or imprisonment.

Lennie's role highlights the vulnerability of people with mental weaknesses in a society where survival depends on using your wits and experience to get by. Lennie is a victim and, without George, would be at the mercy of a social system that values money and power over people and friendship.

Activity 6

Lennie is an innocent who behaves like a child. This is shown partly through his lack of prejudice and partly by his inability to understand the consequences of his actions.

Find the following:

a) two examples of Lennie's lack of prejudice (e.g. against black people and women)

b) two examples of Lennie's inability to realize what will happen as a result of doing **"a bad thing"** (e.g. in Weed and when he kills Curley's wife).

Candy

Key quotations

The door opened and a tall, stoop-shouldered old man came in. He was dressed in blue jeans and he carried a big push-broom in his left hand. [...] He pointed with his right arm, and out of the sleeve came a round stick-like wrist, but no hand. *(Chapter 2)*

Candy is an old man; a former ranch worker who lost his hand in an accident with a machine and is now a **swamper** – someone who cleans out the buildings where the men live. He has an old and smelly dog who is also his only friend. He has a habit, when he is upset or puzzled, of rubbing the stump of his arm either with his other hand or against his stubbly chin. He is envious of the fact that George and Lennie have each other and when he overhears them discussing their dream of the farm he wants to be a part of it. He offers to put in all the money he received as compensation for his accident and it is this gesture that turns the farm from being a dream to a real possibility.

Candy laments the fact that he is too old to be of use for much longer and is fearful of what will happen to him once he can no longer work at all. The fate of his ailing dog is a warning, as Carlson takes it out and shoots it to put it out of its misery. Candy comments: **"When they can me here I wisht somebody'd shoot me. But they won't do nothing like that. I won't have no place to go, an' I can't get no more jobs"** *(Chapter 3)*. This fear is what drives him to trust all of his money to a comparative stranger like George and why he is so bitterly disappointed when his dream is shattered by the death of Curley's wife. He shouts at her dead body in sorrow and anger and repeats the farm story like a **mantra**, his eyes 'blinded with tears' *(Chapter 5)*.

mantra something repeated over as a chant or prayer
swamper a cleaner

Candy buys into the dream of sharing a farm; he knows no one else will look after him when he can't work any more

Activity 7

Make a spider diagram focusing on Candy's role in the novella. Consider how Steinbeck presents Candy:

a) as a gossip talking about other characters

b) as the owner and friend of the old dog

c) as a symbol of old age and weakness

d) as the person who could make the dream farm happen

e) as the would-be champion of Crooks

f) any other functions you think of.

For each idea you include, add a detailed reference or quotation as evidence.

Candy has little time for Curley or his wife. He tells George that Curley is a good boxer and likes to pick on big men. He also tells George to look out for Curley's wife, describing her as **"a tart"** (Chapter 2). When Lennie and Candy are in Crooks's room and she comes in, Candy gets angry with her but is able to resist her taunts by putting his faith in his plans for the future. The dream-turned-plan gives him some self-esteem.

Candy is a passive character, seemingly unable to make things happen for himself. He allows Carlson to shoot his dog, although it was his only friend. He agrees to help George by 'discovering' the body of Curley's wife when George is a distance away, so that he won't be implicated in Lennie's crime. He sympathizes with Lennie but he is also sorry for himself, because he knows his last chance of having a comfortable old age with companionship has gone. The last we see of him is when **'Old Candy lay down in the hay and covered his eyes with his arm'** (Chapter 6).

His function in the novella is to show the hardship endured by those too old and weak to work. His disability and age (like that of his dog) are treated with contempt, as he (like his dog) is perceived as a creature that has long outlived its usefulness.

Activity 8

Imagine you are Candy. Write about how you found the body of Curley's wife and what her death meant to you. You could include:

- some background about your life on the farm and the accident
- your opinions and warnings to George and Lennie about Curley's wife
- the loss of the dream farm and what it means for you
- your fears about being 'canned'
- why you shouted at her dead body.

Curley's wife

> **Key quotations**
>
> A girl was standing there looking in. She had full, rouged lips and wide-spaced eyes, heavily made up. Her fingernails were red. Her hair hung in little rolled clusters, like sausages. She wore a cotton house dress and red mules, on the insteps of which were little bouquets of red ostrich feathers. "I'm lookin' for Curley," she said. Her voice had a nasal, brittle quality. (Chapter 2)

It is obvious from the make-up and red mules that Curley's wife is out of place on a ranch. Her appearance suggests a **scarlet woman**. She seems to be on the ranch as a trophy wife for Curley to show off. She is not even given a name but instead is treated like a possession, belonging to her husband. The ranch hands avoid her, knowing that Curley will get them sacked if he even suspects they are interested in his wife. To Candy she is "a tart" *(Chapter 2)* and George regards her as "jail bait" *(Chapter 2)*. To Lennie she is "purty" *(Chapter 2)* and he admires her, which is a clear cause of tension throughout the narrative.

> **scarlet woman** a promiscuous woman or a prostitute

Despite the mistrust that George and Candy show towards Curley's wife, Steinbeck also reveals that she is very young and naïve – a girl who dreams, like so many others at the time, of being 'discovered' and whisked away to Hollywood. She tells Lennie the story: "'Nother time I met a guy, an' he was in pitchers. Went out to the Riverside Dance Palace with him. He says he was gonna put me in the movies. Says I was a natural. Soon's he got back to Hollywood he was gonna write to me about it" *(Chapter 5)*. It is clear to the reader that this would never happen – her idea of acting is an absurd grand gesture and her "nasal" voice, now that talking films were in fashion, is not really suitable. She is deceiving herself, but nobody else.

Curley's wife is under the naïve illusion that she could have been a movie star

Activity 9

1. Take a sheet of paper and write the heading 'The Impossible Dream' at the top. Divide the rest of the sheet into two columns with the subheadings 'George and Lennie' on the left and 'Curley's wife' on the right. Add the following notes to each column:

   - what the dream is

   - why the dream is important to the characters

   - what makes it impossible

   - how it adds to the tragic aspect of the novella.

2. In your opinion, who is the worst off? Write two or three paragraphs exploring this topic. Justify your point of view with reference to the text.

Curley's wife is a sad and lonely character, unable to speak to a man without flirting. She married Curley in an attempt to show her independence after she convinced herself that her mother had ruined her hopes of achieving stardom. She has only been married for two weeks and is already regretting her hasty decision. Curley still behaves as if he is single, going into town to the brothel with the other men. When he is at home he is bad-tempered.

> **Key quotations**
>
> "Sure I gotta husban'. You all seen him. Swell guy, ain't he? Spends all his time sayin' what he's gonna do to guys he don't like, and he don't like nobody" *(Chapter 4).*

Curley's wife is lonely and an outcast, but while she is undoubtedly a victim of her circumstances, she is also guilty of treating others unfairly and taking her frustrations out on those weaker than herself. She intrudes on Crooks's room without being invited and then scorns Crooks, Candy and Lennie, calling them **"a bunch of bindle stiffs – a nigger an' a dum-dum and a lousy ol' sheep"** *(Chapter 4).* When Crooks tries to make her leave his room she threatens him with lynching. She seems to have little sympathy for other people. This lack of sympathy extends to animals too. When she finds Lennie with the dead puppy she tells him it's just **"a mutt"** *(Chapter 5)* and that there are plenty more of them.

Activity 10

There are three main appearances by Curley's wife in the book:

- **Chapter 2:** from 'A girl was standing there...' to '...and she hurried away'
- **Chapter 4:** from 'Looking in was Curley's wife...' to '...disappeared into the dark barn'
- **Chapter 5:** from 'Curley's wife came around...' to '...for Lennie had broken her neck'.

Examine these three extracts carefully.

1. Complete the following tasks for each extract:

   a) Find two or three words or phrases the narrator uses to influence the reader.

   b) Find two or three things that Curley's wife says that influence the reader.

   c) Find two or three things that Curley's wife does that influence the reader.

   d) Find two or three reactions to Curley's wife from other characters that influence the reader.

2. Use your findings to answer the following question, in two or three paragraphs including quotations: How is Curley's wife presented and how does Steinbeck make the reader feel about her?

When Curley's wife meets Lennie in the barn, she knows she has a captive audience: **'And then her words tumbled out in a passion of communication, as though she hurried before her listener could be taken away'** *(Chapter 5)*. She and Lennie discover a shared liking for stroking soft things, which results in Lennie's most disastrous petting episode.

Her function in the novella is to show the place allotted to women in a society which works on the basis of the 'survival of the fittest'. She is the opposite of Lennie's Aunt Clara, who seems to have been a motherly person who looked after Lennie and fed him home cooking.

Activity 11

Imagine you are Curley's wife. Write a letter to your mother explaining what life is like for you on the ranch. Try to imitate her way of speaking and her tone of being hard done by. You should use what you learn about her in the story, the reaction of the men and her own words and actions as a guide.

You might include the following:

- her thoughts about how the ranch hands behave

- a description of the two new men – George and Lennie – and her feelings about them

- what her husband is like and how lonely life is

- reproach towards her mother for not preventing the marriage and for spoiling her ambitions of being an actress.

Slim

Slim is the real authority on the ranch because the other men respect him. Steinbeck describes his eyes as 'calm' and 'Godlike' *(Chapter 3)*. He is a good judge of character, realizing early on that Lennie isn't "mean" *(Chapter 3)* despite doing "bad things" *(Chapter 1)*. George trusts Slim even though he has only recently met him, which shows how dependable he is. Despite his position of seniority on the ranch, which suggests the ranch hands look up to him, Slim is described in terms of goodness. The words used to show his expression and speech when we first meet him are 'kindly', 'gentle' and 'friendly' *(Chapter 2)*. When Slim supports Carlson over the shooting of Candy's dog, Candy gives up and allows his old friend to be killed. However, it is Slim who tells Carlson to take a shovel, so he can bury the dog and prevent Candy from having to do it.

Activity 12

1. Study the key quotation about Slim in the box below. Find words and phrases that show how Steinbeck makes him different from the other men on the ranch. You should think about the following:

   - Slim's physical appearance
   - the way he carries himself – his manner
   - the narrator's words and phrases that show he is in command
   - the narrator's comments about his level of understanding.

2. Look at the way Steinbeck structures the description. At what point do we find out who the man is? What does Steinbeck tell us before identifying Slim? How does this structure help the reader to form an impression of the character? Write down your ideas in two or three paragraphs, including quotations.

Key quotations

A tall man stood in the doorway. He held a crushed Stetson hat under his arm while he combed his long, black, damp hair straight back. Like the others he wore blue jeans and a short denim jacket. When he had finished combing his hair he moved into the room, and he moved with a majesty only achieved by royalty and master craftsmen. He was a jerkline skinner, the prince of the ranch, capable of driving ten, sixteen, even twenty mules with a single line to the leaders. He was capable of killing a fly on the wheeler's butt with a bull whip without touching the mule. There was a gravity in his manner and a quiet so profound that all talk stopped when he spoke. His authority was so great that his word was taken on any subject, be it politics or love. This was Slim, the jerkline skinner. His hatchet face was ageless. He might have been thirty-five or fifty. His ear heard more than was said to him, and his slow speech had overtones not of thought, but of understanding beyond thought. His hands, large and lean, were as delicate in their action as those of a temple dancer. *(Chapter 2)*

At the end of the story, Slim is the only character who appears to understand what George has done and why. He tells George: "You hadda, George, I swear you hadda" *(Chapter 6)*. He leads George away for a drink while the others just look puzzled.

Slim's function in the novella is to act as a **confidant** for George so we find out more about him and Lennie. He also acts as a friend to George at the end of the narrative and perhaps helps the reader to fully understand his actions. He is presented as a contrast to most of the ranch hands with their lack of sympathy and violent manners.

Activity 13

One of the ways in which Steinbeck presents his characters is through dialogue. Work with a partner to look at the conversation between Slim and George in the first six pages of Chapter 3. Read the dialogue aloud, each playing one of the characters.

1. What do you notice about the length of Slim's speeches compared with George's?

2. What do you notice about the frequency of Slim's speeches?

3. How much of what Slim says is in the form of:

   - questions

   - prompts to get George to carry on talking

   - comments about Lennie?

4. Using your answers to Questions 1–3, write two or three paragraphs explaining how Steinbeck's use of dialogue helps to influence your impression of Slim's character.

Tips for assessment

The way in which characters interact through dialogue is one method that Steinbeck uses to present them. You should always think about this when writing about characters and show how what they say affects your view of them.

Crooks

Crooks is the only black man on the ranch and has his own room because of this. He turns this into an advantage by refusing others entrance to his room unless they are invited. He is called Crooks because of his deformity – caused by a kick from a horse – which causes him pain all the time, despite his constant use of **liniment**. He tells Lennie: **"You go on get outta my room. I ain't wanted in the bunk house, and you ain't wanted in my room"** *(Chapter 4)*. Lennie doesn't understand about segregation and finally Crooks invites him in, secretly pleased to have someone to talk to.

confidant somebody who is entrusted with secrets

liniment a rub that generates heat for soothing aching muscles and bones

Key quotations

The room was swept and fairly neat, for Crooks was a proud, aloof man. He kept his distance and demanded that other people keep theirs. His body was bent over to the left by his crooked spine, and his eyes lay deep in his head, and because of their depths seemed to glitter with intensity. His lean face was lined with deep black wrinkles, and he had thin, pain-tightened lips which were lighter than his face. *(Chapter 4)*

Crooks takes a perverse pleasure in taunting Lennie with the thought that George will not return, finally finding someone in a weaker position than himself. When Lennie gets angry, Crooks explains that he was only trying to show how lonely his life is: "S'pose you didn't have nobody. S'pose you couldn't go into the bunk house and play rummy 'cause you was black. How'd you like that?" *(Chapter 4)*. He laughs at Lennie's dream, saying he's heard the same thing from hundreds of men and it never happens, but when Candy confirms that it is a real plan, with possibilities, he is won over and offers to do odd jobs for nothing if they will count him in. He back-tracks on this, however, when Curley's wife insults and threatens him thereby restoring his position of inferiority.

Crooks's function in the novella is to show the position of black workers at the time and how their lives were lonelier and harsher than itinerant white workers.

Activity 14

1. Look at the first ten pages of Chapter 4, when Lennie visits Crooks in his room. Discuss the following:
   - what this scene tells us about Crooks and the way he lives
   - what it tells us about Lennie
   - whether there are similarities and differences in their situations
   - what reason Crooks might have to torment Lennie when he is glad of his company
   - why you think Steinbeck included this scene.

2. Look at the speech of the two men. What differences do you notice in:

   a) what they say

   b) how they say it?

3. Make notes for revision using your answers to Questions 1 and 2. What does this add to our understanding of their characters? Remember to include evidence from the text to support your ideas.

Activity 15

Write brief notes on what each of the following quotations tells us about Crooks. Remember to focus closely on the use of language and what it reveals about his attitudes towards the society in which he lives.

a)

> "You got no right to come in my room. This here's my room. Nobody got any right in here but me." *(Crooks, Chapter 4)*

b)

> "I was born right here in California. My old man had a chicken ranch, 'bout ten acres. The white kids come to play at our place..." *(Crooks, Chapter 4)*

c)

> "Want me ta tell ya what'll happen? They'll take ya to the booby hatch. They'll tie ya up with a collar, like a dog." *(Crooks, Chapter 4)*

d)

> Crooks had reduced himself to nothing. There was no personality, no ego – nothing to arouse either like or dislike. He said, "Yes, ma'am," and his voice was toneless. *(Chapter 4)*

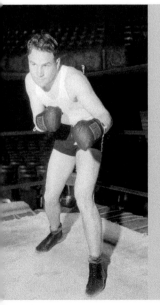

Two-time world champion Jimmy McLarnin poses in a boxing stance in Los Angeles, California, 1933. Boxing was a popular sport in the USA in the 1930s

Curley

Curley's first action when he sees Lennie is to go into a boxing stance. 'His arms gradually bent at the elbows and his hands closed into fists. He stiffened and went into a slight crouch. His glance was at once calculating and pugnacious' *(Chapter 2)*. Candy tells them that Curley is a boxer and that he likes to pick on big guys. He suggests it's because Curley is a little man. He is one of the "mean little guys" *(Chapter 2)*, in all senses, since he uses his position as the boss's son to bully others. He seems to have an inferiority complex about his size and feels he has to assert his masculinity at all times. In his eyes this amounts to fighting and aggression. Slim uses Curley's fear of being laughed at to persuade him not to get Lennie the sack after his hand is crushed.

Curley is a jealous husband, always suspecting the ranch hands of trying it on with his wife, although this doesn't prevent him from going to the local brothel with the men on Saturday night. He treats his wife as a possession, rather than as another human being, and as another way to prove his masculinity, which we can see in the way he tells people about his glove being full of Vaseline. When the men find his wife's body, Curley is more interested in going after Lennie with a shotgun than in grieving for her. He refuses to stay with her when Slim suggests it, saying, **"I'm gonna shoot the guts outta that big bastard myself, even if i only got one hand. i'm gonna get 'im"** *(Chapter 5)*. It seems his revenge is as much for what Lennie did to him as for his wife's murder. He has no redeeming qualities at all and his function in the novella is to create a situation where we know Lennie has no hope of mercy.

Curley also represents the abuse of power. His power comes partly from his father, as the owner of the ranch, and partly from his prowess as a boxer, so he can – and does – use both of these to assert himself over others. Curley is dominating over his wife and, although we never see them together, we see the effects of his jealousy and we see her reaction when Slim tells her of Curley's whereabouts: **'She was suddenly apprehensive'** [...] **'and she hurried away'** *(Chapter 2)*. Curley seems quite unable to relate to other people, seeing them only as either stronger or weaker than himself.

Activity 16

1. Find quotations from the text to support the following points:
   - Curley is a very good boxer *(Chapters 2 or 3)*.
   - Curley always picks on men who are bigger than he is *(Chapter 2)*.
   - Since his marriage Curley has got even cockier *(Chapter 2)*.
   - Curley is possessive of his wife *(Chapters 2 or 3)*.

2. Write two paragraphs showing what your chosen quotations reveal about Curley and his role in the novella.

Tips for assessment

Upgrade

An essential part of characterization is the way in which characters interact and the relationships they have. You should consider how characters affect each other by the decisions they make and the actions they take.

Character map

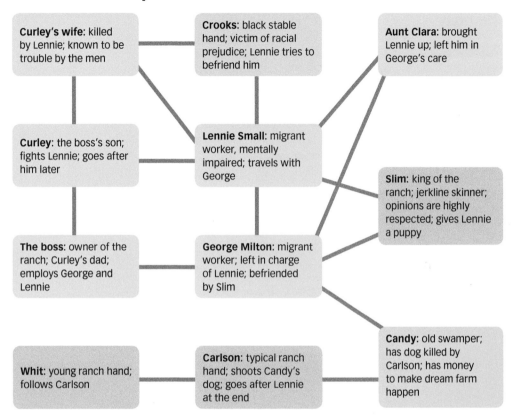

Curley's wife: killed by Lennie; known to be trouble by the men

Crooks: black stable hand; victim of racial prejudice; Lennie tries to befriend him

Aunt Clara: brought Lennie up; left him in George's care

Curley: the boss's son; fights Lennie; goes after him later

Lennie Small: migrant worker, mentally impaired; travels with George

Slim: king of the ranch; jerkline skinner; opinions are highly respected; gives Lennie a puppy

The boss: owner of the ranch; Curley's dad; employs George and Lennie

George Milton: migrant worker; left in charge of Lennie; befriended by Slim

Candy: old swamper; has dog killed by Carlson; has money to make dream farm happen

Whit: young ranch hand; follows Carlson

Carlson: typical ranch hand; shoots Candy's dog; goes after Lennie at the end

Character map key

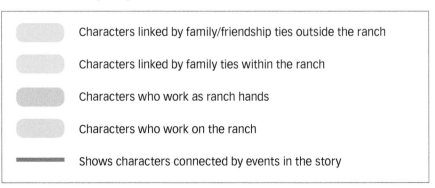

Characters linked by family/friendship ties outside the ranch

Characters linked by family ties within the ranch

Characters who work as ranch hands

Characters who work on the ranch

Shows characters connected by events in the story

Minor characters

The boss

> **Key quotations**
>
> A little stocky man stood in the open doorway [...] he wore high-heeled boots and spurs to prove he was not a laboring man. *(Chapter 2)*

The boss only appears on one occasion when he first decides to employ George and Lennie, but he asks searching questions and seems annoyed that they are late. He accuses George of exploiting Lennie for his own gain.

It is his function to show what other people might think about the relationship between George and Lennie. It also shows the distance between the ranch owners and the men they employ, as well as the lack of genuine interest in them as human beings. His action in providing whisky at Christmas is seen as generous, but there is no mention of him joining them for a drink.

Carlson

Carlson is descibed as a 'powerful, big-stomached man' *(Chapter 2)*. He is a typical ranch hand and lacks imagination although he is not unsympathetic. He makes a joke about Lennie's name being Small, which amuses him. He can't bear the smell of Candy's old dog in the bunk house and suggests that the dog should be shot and that Candy should have one of Slim's puppies instead: "Look, Candy. This ol' dog jus' suffers hisself all the time. If you was to take him out and shoot him right in the back of the head –" he leaned over and pointed "– right there, why he'd never know what hit him" *(Chapter 3)*. This is a lesson learned by George who uses it at the end of the book, when he shoots Lennie. Carlson offers to shoot the dog himself with his Luger pistol and when Slim backs him up, Candy has no choice but to agree. Carlson is down to earth and wants to save the dog more suffering (as well as relieving them of the smell) but he doesn't consider Candy's feelings about the dog.

When Curley suggests they go after Lennie, Carlson says, "I'll get my Luger" *(Chapter 5)*. We know what this means for Lennie. Carlson is insensitive to the feelings of others, although he is not an unkind or aggressive man. He has the last speech in the book when he asks, as Slim leads George away, "Now what the hell ya suppose is eatin' them two guys?" *(Chapter 6)*.

Carlson's function in the novella is to show a 'typical' ranch hand and act as a contrast to Slim, as he lacks empathy, and to George, as he lacks imagination even for dreams. While not aggressive, like Curley, he is quick to consider using his gun when he thinks it necessary.

Whit

His sloping shoulders were bent forward and he walked heavily on his heels, as though he carried the invisible grain bag. *(Chapter 3)*

Whit only appears twice in the book. The first time is to show the kind of magazine the ranch hands read and to be impressed that a previous migrant worker has had a letter published in one. The second occasion is at the discovery of the dead woman when, lacking a gun, he is sent by Curley into Soledad to fetch the deputy sheriff. He is typical of the migrant labourers who moved from place to place, without ever getting to know people personally. He demonstrates the kind of casual relationships that ranch workers would be used to.

Activity 17

Look at the roles of the boss, Carlson and Whit and complete the following tasks:

a) Write down everything we learn about each character, adding evidence from the text to show how you know it.

b) Are Carlson, the boss and Whit 'proper' characters or are they just representatives of certain 'types'? If the latter, what kind of people do they represent?

c) We never learn a great deal about these characters, so why do you think Steinbeck has chosen to include them? Write two or three paragraphs explaining your views with reference to the text.

Writing about characters

Upgrade

You need to gain an understanding of the characters and their relationships in *Of Mice and Men*. Exam questions may ask you to focus on the role of a particular character. You should aim to cover the following in your answer:

- the kind of things the author gives the character to say

- the kind of things the author gives the character to do

- how other characters react to them

- why the author has included this character in the novella (their role or function)

- how the character is presented – such as the language used to describe them, the character's speech patterns and also parallels between characters.

Dialogue

Understatement and hyperbole

Dialogue is very important in the novella and is used to move on the action, as well as to reveal characters and relationships. The men speak in the way that ranch hands would have done, that is to say, with limited vocabulary and a tendency to swear. Modern readers may be shocked by their use of racist language, such as the use of the term 'nigger', which was common in the USA at the time. To the characters in the story, however, this is just the way they speak, much as George calling Lennie a 'crazy bastard' is actually a term of endearment. The men rarely express affection and this is a way of doing so while also, in a sense, hiding it.

Steinbeck uses **understatement** to show that his characters are not used to expressing feelings of friendship or love. George's statement that *"you get used to goin' around with a guy an' you can't get rid of him" (Chapter 3)* disguises his real feelings that, without Lennie, he'd be alone and miserable and have nothing to plan for, just like the other men. Steinbeck also uses **hyperbole** where things are overstated for effect, as when George tells Lennie, *"Red and blue and green rabbits, Lennie. Millions of 'em" (Chapter 1)*. In this example, George uses hyperbole for comic effect, but his exaggeration also perhaps helps to highlight the unreachable nature of their dream.

> **hyperbole** exaggeration, used to express something strongly for effect and not intended to be taken literally
>
> **understatement** a limited or restrained manner of expressing yourself that leaves a lot unsaid, but implies more than is said

Activity 1

1. Find three examples of understatement from the book, where people mean much more than they actually say. Divide a sheet of paper in two. In one column write down the quotations and next to them, in the second column, write down what it is they leave unsaid.

2. Find three examples of hyperbole, where things are deliberately exaggerated for effect. On the reverse of the paper draw another two columns. Use one column to write down quotations and, in the next column, write down why each use of hyperbole is effective.

3. Discuss and make notes on what you think Steinbeck wanted to achieve by using these techniques.

Characterization

Steinbeck gives his characters different ways of speaking that mark them out. George talks to Lennie like a parent addressing a child: *"Good boy. That's swell. You say that over two, three times so you sure won't forget it" (Chapter 1)*. Lennie relies on George to tell him what to do, even when Curley is hitting him: *"Make 'um stop, George" (Chapter 3)*. Candy's interest in gossip is shown by what he tells George about the ranch and his repeated use of the phrase *"Tell you what..."*. Curley's aggressive nature is reflected in the way he speaks to George when they've only just met: *"By Christ, he's gotta talk when he's spoke to. What the hell are you gettin' into it for?" (Chapter 2)*.

Slim thinks carefully before giving his opinions. He does not make hasty judgements. We learn he has been 'studying' Candy's dog before he agrees that it would be better to shoot it. He also knows how to get rid of Curley's wife without causing offence; he greets her with *"Hi, Good-lookin'" (Chapter 2)* before telling her he's seen Curley going into the house.

Activity 2

1. Work with a partner and look at the conversation between George and Candy about Curley in Chapter 2 from **'George was watching the door'** to **'"That's a dirty thing to tell around"'**. Read it aloud just as it's written in the text.

   Look out for the following:

   - the way Steinbeck juxtaposes actions with the dialogue
   - use of **idioms** like 'slough' and 'canned'
   - use of non-verbal sounds
   - use of implied meanings
   - use of question and answer
   - use of statements that invite more information.

2. Based on your reading of the scene, how does Steinbeck use language to show the characters of the two men? Consider:

   a) what they say

   b) how they say it

   c) what they do.

---

idiom a phrase or expression which has a meaning that is specific to a certain dialect, e.g. 'don't you try to put nothing over', which means 'don't try to cheat me'

Dialect

Dialect is a regional form of speech, common to a particular area. A **dialect** often has its own vocabulary and forms of grammar. It is also linked to class and levels of education in a social sense. The characters in *Of Mice and Men* are labourers; they often struggle to express themselves in words and when they do they use a language that is simple and often repetitive.

> **dialect** a way of speaking that is characteristic of a particular group of people, such as those who live in the same geographical region

The vocabulary in the novella can be hard to understand at times, although some expressions are highly descriptive, such as **"pants rabbits"** *(Chapter 2)* for lice or fleas. Phrases such as **"bum steer"** (false information) *(Chapter 2)*, which suggests steering someone in a wrong direction, and **"got the eye"** (looking at men in a sexual way) *(Chapter 2)* also have a visual power that is arguably lacking in Standard English.

Unfamiliar words and phrases

bucking grain passing full bags of grain along a line of men and onto a cart

candy wagon a type of bus used for transporting people

cat house similar to whorehouse or brothel

graybacks lice

jack-pin a movable pin on a ship around which ropes are fastened

slug a single measure of spirits

Steinbeck was a bindle stiff himself, so was familiar with the dialect workers used. In addition to the use of dialect words, Steinbeck also presents this dialect to the reader through the use of **elision**, as in **"ever'body"**, **"settin"** and **"gonna"**, which allows the reader to 'hear' the characters without obscuring the meaning.

Despite its simplicity, the language of the workers is often rhythmic and poetic. This is especially true when they talk about the farm. The sentences that Steinbeck gives his characters may not be grammatically correct – phrases like **"shouldn't ought to"** and **"we wouldn't ask nobody"** are common – but they do not detract from our understanding; in fact they add to it because they tell us how these men think and what they sound like.

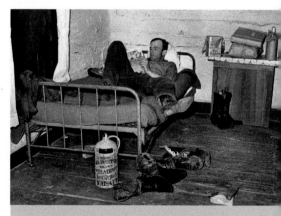

The reality of typical bunk house conditions in 1930s America was a stark contrast to the idealized dream farm

Activity 3

1. Work in a group of six. Each person is responsible for looking at one chapter of the book. For your chapter, find examples of the features of speech listed below and make notes. Your notes should include examples of the words and phrases used, their meaning in Standard English and who uses them.

   a) elision

   b) non-standard grammar (see examples on page 50 as a guide)

   c) different forms of words, like **"jest"** for "just", and **"settin"** for "sitting"

   d) swear words and phrases like **"bastard"**, **"hell"** and **"God damn"**

   e) run-together words like **"oughta"** for "ought to" and **"musta"** for "must have"

   f) use of **double negatives** such as **"wasn't doin' nothin"**

   g) use of idioms or dialect words like **"bindle"** and **"pants rabbits"**.

2. Use your findings to discuss the following questions as a group:

   a) Are there any characters that use certain features more than others?

   b) What does the use of dialogue features reveal about the characters, for example their values, their lifestyle and the society in which they live?

---

double negative using two negative forms together in a phrase or sentence, e.g. 'ain't going nowhere' instead of 'isn't going anywhere'

elision leaving out one or more sounds from a word to make it easier to say

---

Tips for assessment

Try to think about how and why Steinbeck uses dialogue to reveal certain things about each character and his/her role in the novella.

Repetition

Another language technique that Steinbeck uses in the book is repetition. The men often say the same thing more than once. This perhaps gives the reader an impression of their lack of education, but it also helps to reinforce certain ideas, themes and motifs that are important in the text.

The telling of the dream farm story is the most obvious example. Lennie never tires of hearing it and can repeat some of it by heart, which helps us to understand his childlike outlook.

The retelling of the dream, using the same words each time, also helps to give it the tone of a fairy tale, which is appropriate because it will never come true. Also, as happens in such tales, each time it is told it is embellished with extra details, almost as if the men are building the farm with words. At the end of the book the tale is retold to emphasize what they have lost. Candy repeats 'the old words' with tears in his eyes, "An' they'd of been a pig and chickens... an' in the winter... the little fat stove... an' the rain comin'... an' us jus' settin' there" *(Chapter 5)*. George shoots Lennie after telling him about the dream for the last time, now that George knows it is impossible.

The description of the dream farm is repeated so frequently it takes on the tone of a fairy tale

The characters also use repetition within their speech for **rhetorical** effect. For example, Candy says, "I didn't hear nothing you guys was sayin'. I ain't interested in nothing you was sayin'. A guy on a ranch don't never listen nor he don't ast no questions" *(Chapter 2)*. This shows Candy's ability to use the power of everyday speech and the repetition of ideas to convince an audience.

rhetorical expressed in a way designed to persuade or impress the listener

Activity 4

1. Find examples of repetition of the following:

   a) the dream as it is told when we first meet George and Lennie *(Chapter 1)*, when old Candy makes it a possibility *(Chapter 3)* and when George wants Lennie to imagine it before he dies *(Chapter 6)*

   b) the idea that being shot is better than being useless *(Chapter 3)*

   c) rhetorical repetition to persuade a listener *(Chapters 2 and 4)*.

2. Write one or two paragraphs about the use of repetition in the story, including the effect of this on you as a reader. Use quotations as examples.

Description

In contrast to his presentation of dialogue, Steinbeck uses a wider range of vocabulary in his descriptive passages. At the start of the book, for example, he writes about 'sycamores with mottled, white, recumbent limbs and branches that arch over the pool' and also how 'a stilted heron labored up into the air and pounded down river' *(Chapter 1)*. Steinbeck's use of **figurative language** here – a reclining person and a creature on stilts – is well chosen and makes the scene vivid. The description creates a feeling of timelessness and tranquillity and presents a place where people can escape from the world of hard work and aggression. Steinbeck uses similarly detailed imagery at the end of the book to reveal how the setting has become tainted by violence and death.

Steinbeck's choice of words brings the image of the heron and pond to life

figurative language language that uses 'figures of speech' such as metaphors, similes, personification, etc.

The description of the bunk house and the harness room, on the other hand, resemble stage directions in that there is little use of figurative language, e.g. 'In three walls there were small, square windows, and in the fourth, a solid door with a wooden latch' *(Chapter 2)*. The language, like the place, provides a functional setting for the characters to interact with each other.

> **metaphor** a comparison of one thing to another for effect; a metaphor states that one thing is the other, e.g. 'Lennie dabbled his big paw in the water'
>
> **onomatopoeia** words that sound like the things they represent, like the lynch mob 'crashing in the brush'
>
> **pathetic fallacy** using nature to reflect people's moods, as when Curley's wife is lying dead: 'As happens sometimes, a moment settled and hovered and remained for much more than a moment'
>
> **personification** giving human characteristics to inanimate objects, e.g. 'The sycamore leaves whispered in a little night breeze'
>
> **simile** a comparison that shows it is comparing by using 'like' or 'as', e.g. Lennie is shown 'snorting into the water like a horse'

Activity 5

1. Re-read Chapter 6. What effects does Steinbeck achieve through his use of:

   a) **metaphor**

   b) **onomatopoeia**

   c) **pathetic fallacy**

   d) **personification**

   e) **simile**?

2. Compare this chapter with the depiction of another setting in the novella and explain what this reveals about Steinbeck's use of setting.

Atmosphere

Steinbeck uses a mixture of action, dialogue and descriptive language to create atmosphere in the novella.

For example, Steinbeck uses verbs such as 'slashed', 'smashed' and 'slugging' to show Curley's violence, while Lennie is likened to both a tame bear who covers his face 'with his huge paws' and a sheep as he 'bleated with terror'. This contrast, between the actions of Curley and those of Lennie, who is likened to both a tame bear and a sheep, is deliberately set up so that the reader sympathizes with Lennie throughout.

Contrast is a technique that Steinbeck uses throughout the novel to create atmosphere, such as the contrast between light and dark

In addition to description, Steinbeck also creates tension using dialogue. For example, at the end of Chapter 3, Slim and Carlson use emotionally charged phrases, weighted with oaths and threats to fend off Curley: "your own God damn wife", "lay offa me", "you God damn punk", "I'll kick your God damn head off". Steinbeck then contrasts this dialogue with the language he uses to describe Lennie 'smiling with delight at the memory of the ranch'. The reader knows immediately that Lennie is an easy target for Curley.

In the final chapter of the book, Steinbeck creates tension by interspersing the dialogue with descriptions of the noise made by the men as they search for Lennie.

Key quotations

The voices came close now. George raised the gun and listened to the voices.

Lennie begged, "Le's do it now. Le's get that place now."

"Sure, right now. I gotta. We gotta." *(Chapter 6)*

For George and for the reader, his words hold a significance that Lennie cannot comprehend, as Lennie does not see the gun.

The shooting of Lennie is told in plain language that makes it as shocking as it should be, although the sentences are carefully balanced so they reflect the deliberate nature of George's actions.

Key quotations

And George raised the gun and steadied it, and he brought the muzzle of it close to the back of Lennie's head. The hand shook violently, but his face set and his hand steadied. He pulled the trigger. The crash of the shot rolled up the hills and rolled down again. Lennie jarred, and then settled slowly forward to the sand, and he lay without quivering. *(Chapter 6)*

The adverb 'violently' describes both the shaking of George's hand and the action it is about to commit. The whole killing is described in 'real time' so that the reader sees the actions as they happen, which makes it immediate, and it is told from George's viewpoint, which makes the reader part of it.

Activity 6

1. Re-read Chapter 5, which begins: **'One end of the great barn…'.** Make notes on the ways in which Steinbeck uses language to build tension in this chapter from the first mention of Lennie in the barn up to the point where he kills Curley's wife. You should include the following:

   a) some of the phrases Lennie uses when speaking to the dead puppy

   b) the words and phrases Curley's wife uses to persuade Lennie to talk to her

   c) the phrases the author uses to make us aware of the horseshoe tournament happening outside the barn

   d) the words and phrases that Lennie uses to explain his love of petting things

   e) Lennie's speech as he tries to stop Curley's wife struggling.

2. Based on your notes, write two or three paragraphs explaining how Steinbeck uses language to build suspense and create tension in this chapter.

Irony

Steinbeck uses irony to involve the reader and to make the reader think about important themes and ideas in the book. He uses this technique in different ways.

dramatic irony a literary technique by which the significance of a character's words or actions is clear to the audience or reader but not to the character

situational irony created when there is a difference between what is expected to happen and what actually happens; or where what actually happens is deliberately different to what is expected

Situational irony

Here are some examples of **situational irony**.

- George kills Lennie because he loves him.
- Candy, physically the weakest man on the ranch, can make the dream possible.
- Lennie's love for animals leads to them dying.
- Curley and his wife are always looking for each other but never stay together.

Dramatic irony

The list below includes some examples of **dramatic irony**.

- The behaviour of Curley's wife around the men versus the reader's knowledge of what the men think of her.
- Curley's wife's decision to persuade Lennie to stroke her hair versus the reader's knowledge of what usually happens when Lennie pets things.
- The men's belief that Lennie has Carlson's gun versus the reader's knowledge that George has it.

Activity 7

Look at each list of examples under 'Irony'. Add more examples of your own. Why do you think Steinbeck uses the device of irony in the novella? Why is it effective?

Biblical parallels

Steinbeck's use of language in *Of Mice and Men* is influenced by biblical references and biblical imagery. He uses this to draw attention to particular ideas and also to prompt a specific emotional response in the reader.

Here are some key examples.

- The story of the dream farm is similar to a parable, where the farm itself stands for heaven. As Crooks points out: "Just like heaven. Ever'body wants a little piece of lan'. I read plenty of books out here. Nobody never gets to heaven, and nobody gets no land" *(Chapter 4)*. Lennie's actions mean that heaven becomes impossible.
- The retelling of the story of the dream farm is like a religious **rite**. Candy, in particular, regards it as a possible chance of redemption. "Maybe if I give you guys my money, you'll let me hoe in the garden even after I ain't no good at it. An' I'll wash dishes an' little chicken stuff like that. But I'll be on our own place, an' I'll be let to work on our own place" *(Chapter 3)*.

rite a custom or practice performed as a means of showing faith in a belief

- Steinbeck makes a subtle comparison between the scene by the pool and the Garden of **Eden**.

- He presents George and Lennie like humans after the fall, when Adam and Eve were condemned to roam the earth and till the soil: "Guys like us, that work on ranches, are the loneliest guys in the world. They got no family. They don't belong no place" *(Chapter 1)*.

In the Bible, Adam and Eve were banished by God from the Garden of Eden to live a life of toil and hardship

Eden the idyllic garden in which Adam and Eve lived before they were banished for disobeying God

Activity 8

1. Look at each passage below. Passage 1 is from the *King James Bible* and Passage 2 is from *Of Mice and Men*. Note down any similarities that you notice and also the key differences. If you can, read each passage aloud and pay particular attention to the descriptive words, the length of the sentences and the number of **clauses** and **phrases**.

> Passage 1: *King James Bible*
> **And the LORD God planted a garden eastward in Eden; and there he put the man whom he had formed. And out of the ground made the LORD God to grow every tree that is pleasant to the sight, and good for food; the tree of life also in the midst of the garden, and the tree of knowledge of good and evil. And a river went out of Eden to water the garden.** *(Genesis 1:2)*

> Passage 2: *Of Mice and Men*
> **On one side of the river the golden foothill slopes curve up to the strong and rocky Gabilan mountains, but on the valley side the water is lined with trees – willows fresh and green with every spring, carrying in their lower leaf junctures the debris of the winter's flooding; and sycamores with mottled, white, recumbent limbs and branches that arch over the pool.** *(Chapter 1)*

2. Did you note any similarities? What effect do these parallels have on the overall impact of the second passage?

> **clause** a part of a sentence that could form a sentence on its own
>
> **phrase** a group of words in a sentence that could not form a separate sentence

Writing about language

Upgrade

Whatever you are asked to focus on in your assessment, you should pay close attention to how Steinbeck uses language to create effects and present ideas. You should show your awareness of the ways in which Steinbeck uses language to create and sustain atmosphere in the novella, such as how he creates suspense or drama. You should also be able to write about how he uses dialogue in conjunction with descriptive language.

Men and nature

Steinbeck was awarded the Nobel Prize for Literature in 1962. The extract below is taken from a speech by Anders Osterling, Secretary of the Swedish Academy, as he presented Steinbeck with the award.

> "His sympathies always go out to the oppressed, to the misfits and the distressed; he likes to contrast the simple joy of life with the brutal and cynical craving for money. But in him we find the American temperament also in his great feeling for nature, for the tilled soil, the wasteland, the mountains, and the ocean coasts, all an inexhaustible source of inspiration to Steinbeck in the midst of, and beyond, the world of human beings."

In *Of Mice and Men* Steinbeck considers the relationship between people and nature through the way he presents the characters' attitudes to the land and to animals. George dreams of owning land which he can plant and sow and reap, as people have done for many centuries.

Key quotations

"If I was bright, if I was even a little bit smart, I'd have my own little place, an' I'd be bringin' in my own crops, 'stead of doin' all the work and not getting what comes up outta the ground." *(George, Chapter 3)*

Activity 1

1. Find three examples from the novella that help to show:

   a) how working for others on the ranch is presented

   b) how working on your own piece of land is presented.

2. Discuss what your examples reveal about attitudes to working on the land. Create a visual display, which is divided into two, showing men working for others and men working their own land. You could include pictures, quotations from the text and your own comments. Write a brief summary underneath about why you think Steinbeck chose to make these ideas central to his book.

The men have a working relationship with animals which is unsentimental and practical. Slim drowns several puppies when they are born because he knows their mother won't be able to feed them. However, he cares for his mules and horses because they are valuable for farm work. Carlson shows no hesitation before shooting Candy's old dog which can no longer work as a sheepdog and, like Candy himself, is no longer able to be of real use. Candy is upset by this, having reared the dog from a puppy. He later tells George he should have done it himself as a last favour for his old companion. This shows that, deep down, he understands why the dog was put down. He says: "When they can me here I wisht somebody'd shoot me" *(Chapter 3)*. This shirking of his final responsibility to his old friend has an effect on George when he has to do the same thing for Lennie at the end of the book.

The men rarely form close friendships and have unsentimental relationships with animals

Land and livestock form the basis of the farm that George and Lennie dream of. They want to plant crops and farm animals – and of course keep rabbits, for Lennie. Lennie's relationship with animals is simple – he just wants to pet them, although their deaths don't seem to affect him much. His only concern is that George will be cross and not let him tend the rabbits. He is thrilled to be given one of Slim's puppies, but cannot resist petting it to death.

Activity 2

Imagine you have been asked to contribute a two-minute slot to a radio programme about *Of Mice and Men* on the theme of 'man and nature'. Work with a partner to prepare the following:

a) a discussion of the theme and its importance in the novella

b) three short readings from the book which illustrate points made in your discussion.

Find some suitable music to start and end your contribution to the programme, then record it.

Loneliness

The novella is set near the town of Soledad, which means 'solitude' in Spanish. This is very apt because loneliness is an important theme throughout the book. Nearly every character in the book is portrayed as lonely or, at best, alone. George's story about the dream farm always begins: **"Guys like us, that work on ranches, are the loneliest guys in the world. They got no family. They don't belong no place"** *(Chapter 1)*. Steinbeck shows this through characters like Whit, who is thrilled to find a published letter from a man who had moved on some months before. Also Candy speaks of the ranch hand who occupied George's bunk previously, saying that he'd **"just quit, the way a guy will"** *(Chapter 2)*. Steinbeck depicts the men as rootless, going from place to place to find work wherever they can.

Lonely, rootless ranch workers travelled from place to place to find work

By travelling together, George and Lennie are the exceptions, and this gives rise to curiosity in some and suspicion in others. The boss suspects George of exploiting Lennie, while Curley accuses them of being more than friends. Even Slim thinks it's **"funny"**.

> **Key quotations**
>
> "I hardly never seen two guys travel together. You know how the hands are, they just come in and get their bunk and work a month, and then they quit and go out alone. Never seem to give a damn about nobody." *(Slim, Chapter 3)*

Candy

Candy is lonely, more so since he can't do the same work as the men and so is not treated as an 'equal'. His old sheepdog is his only companion, which is why he is so reluctant to see it put down. This loneliness explains why he is so anxious to help George and Lennie buy the dream farm – to the point where he will put in his life's savings, even though they have only just met. Steinbeck shows Candy's desperation when they discover the body of Curley's wife: **'Now Candy spoke his greatest fear. "You an' me can get that little place, can't we, George? You an' me can go there an' live nice, can't we, George? Can't we?"** *(Chapter 5)*. Even as he speaks these words he knows that one of the consequences of the killing will be the loneliness and solitude that both he and George cannot escape. Without Lennie, George will become like all the others.

Key quotations

"I'll work my month an' I'll take my fifty bucks an' I'll stay all night in some lousy cat house. Or I'll set in some poolroom till ever'body goes home. An' then I'll come back an' work another month an' I'll have fifty bucks more." *(George, Chapter 5)*

Activity 3

Look at the key quotation above. Compare it with what George says in Chapter 1, below:

Key quotations

"God a'mighty, if I was alone I could live so easy. I could go get a job an' work, an' no trouble. No mess at all, and when the end of the month come I could take my fifty bucks and go into town and get whatever I want. Why, I could stay in a cat house all night. I could eat any place I want, hotel or any place, and order any damn thing I could think of. An' I could do all that every damn month. Get a gallon of whisky, or set in a pool room and play cards or shoot pool." *(George, Chapter 1)*

a) How has Steinbeck changed the tone of what George says? Think about the way in which the same scene is presented each time. Select the words and phrases that suggest George sees this as a good outcome in Chapter 1 but a poor one in Chapter 5.

b) Decide what this tells us about George's relationship with Lennie. Write two or three paragraphs explaining your ideas with references to the text.

Crooks

Crooks, the stable buck, is lonely because of his colour. He cannot mix with the other men, except at Christmas or to play horseshoes with them, because of prejudice. This isolation has forced him into a position of bitter pride, which is shown when Lennie intrudes on him: "I seen it over an' over – a guy talkin' to another guy and it don't make no difference if he don't hear or understand. The thing is, they're talkin', or they're settin' still not talkin'. It don't make no difference, no difference" *(Chapter 4)*. The need for company is what makes Crooks open up to Lennie. For a brief moment he is swept up into offering to help the men to secure their own place. However, after he is threatened by Curley's wife and shunned by George, he tells Candy to forget he ever wanted to be part of the plan.

Activity 4

Discuss why Steinbeck decided to include the brief moment when Crooks becomes involved in plans to secure the dream farm.

What does his quick withdrawal from the plan make you think?

Curley's wife

For all her flirting and her meanness, Curley's wife is also a lonely person. Living on the ranch among a group of single men who steer clear of her and with a husband who only talks about himself, she is quite isolated. Although she has only been married for two weeks, she is bored and restless, and this leads to her hanging around the men's quarters and trying to engage them in conversation. She finds Lennie to be a good listener. She says to him: **"Wha's the matter with me?" [...] "Ain't I got a right to talk to nobody? Whatta they think I am anyways? You're a nice guy. I don't know why I can't talk to you. I ain't doin' no harm to you"** *(Chapter 5)*. She has no female company and the men regard her with hostility and suspicion.

Activity 5

1. In groups of three, prepare a dramatization of the theme of loneliness by writing a short **monologue** for each of the characters below. Try to include suitable quotations from the book.

   a) Candy

   b) Crooks

   c) Curley's wife

2. Consider how you would stage your dramatic piece in order to emphasize the loneliness of each character. Write stage directions to show this.

monologue a long speech spoken by a character, usually reflecting on his/her internal thoughts and feelings

Tips for assessment

To access the higher marks when writing about a theme, such as loneliness, you need to think about how it relates to the context of the book. For example: how the lack of work caused by the Great Depression made so many men travel away from their families to find jobs; how the Jim Crow laws forced separation on black Americans which was especially hard in California where the black population was so small; or how the lack of welfare provision made older workers desperate not to be sacked.

Power and responsibility

The connection between power and responsibility is a prominent theme throughout the novella. Steinbeck explores this theme through the way he presents the characters and their relationships.

The boss

The boss is the most powerful man on the ranch, but he only appears once. He has the power to sack or "can" the workers if they do not pull their weight. He does not, however, have the power to stop the men moving on when they wish.

Slim

Slim is held in respect because of his skills and wisdom, and uses his position to make fair judgements.

Curly is a bully who thinks that fighting is the way to prove his power

Curley

Curley, as the boss's son, is also a figure of power, but uses it irresponsibly to bully and intimidate others. He cannot be 'canned' like the other men but he could see to it that the other men are sacked if they offend him. This is what George fears when Lennie crushes Curley's hand, but Slim protects them. Curley uses his position, as a jealous husband, to ensure the men are wary of speaking to his wife, thus worsening her isolation.

Curley's wife

Curley's wife has some power, both in her role as the boss's daughter-in-law and in her portrayal as a **femme fatale**. She tries to use sexual attraction to gain attention from the men, although it doesn't work with anyone except Lennie. She uses her power as a white woman to silence Crooks when he tries to order her out of his room and she uses her position on the ranch to insult the three men she finds in Crooks's room, saying "They left all the weak ones here" (Chapter 4). Her assessment is accurate because Candy, Crooks and Lennie are the weak members of this society.

> **femme fatale** a French phrase that is applied to any woman who has supposedly fatal powers of sexual attraction

Activity 6

Look at the quotations below. Discuss what they tell you about power in the novella. Write two or three paragraphs explaining your ideas.

a)

All right. But don't try to put nothing over, 'cause you can't get away with nothing. I seen wise guys before. *(The boss, Chapter 2)*

b)

By Christ, he's gotta talk when he's spoke to. What the hell are you gettin' into it for? *(Curley, Chapter 2)*

c)

Carl's right, Candy. That dog ain't no good to himself. I wisht somebody'd shoot me if I got old an' a cripple. *(Slim, Chapter 3)*

d)

Well, you keep your place then, Nigger. I could get you strung up on a tree so easy it ain't even funny. *(Curley's wife, Chapter 4)*

Candy

Candy has less power than the other ranch workers because he is old and injured and can no longer work as they can. He does, however, have the financial power to help make the dream farm a possibility.

Crooks

Despite being the best educated man on the ranch, Crooks is an outcast as a result of racist policies that force him to live separately from the other workers.

Lennie

Lennie is picked on by Curley, who wants to prove how 'big' he is by fighting him, and by Curley's wife, who responds to Lennie's innocence. Even Crooks bullies Lennie, making him aware of his dependence on George. However, Crooks realizes the risk he is taking just in time: 'Crooks saw the danger as it approached him. He edged back on his bunk to get out of the way. "I was just supposin'," he said. "George ain't hurt. He's all right. He'll be back all right" *(Chapter 4)*. Lennie's physical strength gives him power over other people and over animals, but it is always destructive because his mental weakness makes him unable to use it with restraint.

George

George can hold his own both physically and mentally – we see Curley assess him and move on to Lennie who is physically strong but mentally weak. Although George has little economic power because he has no money, he does have power in his friendship with Lennie. He admits to having used his power over Lennie for his own amusement in the past, telling Lennie to jump into the river when he couldn't swim, but he is now responsible and tries to protect Lennie from the consequences of his actions.

Carlson

Carlson has his strength and his ability with a gun to ensure he is independent of men like Curley. However, Steinbeck also presents him as a man without the ambition or imagination to wish to better his circumstances.

George has the respect of others on the ranch because he is physically and mentally capable

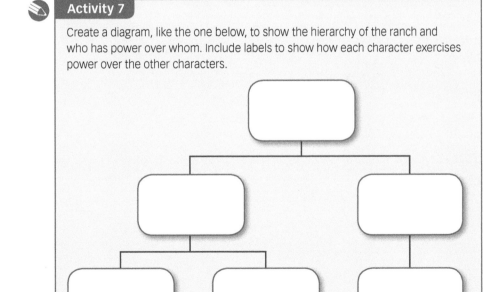

Activity 7

Create a diagram, like the one below, to show the hierarchy of the ranch and who has power over whom. Include labels to show how each character exercises power over the other characters.

Activity 8

Work in a small group of three to five people and create a series of tableaux, or freeze frames, to illustrate the following:

- Curley's misuse of power to bully and intimidate
- Crooks's power to frighten Lennie
- Curley's wife's power to intimidate Crooks
- George's power over Lennie
- Lennie's power because of his physical strength.

Stage each freeze frame in turn, holding each one for five seconds. One person in the group should explain the choices behind the freeze frame.

If you have time, you could look up suitable quotations for one or more characters in the scene to show how Steinbeck presents each power relationship.

Dreams and plans

The 'American Dream' is essentially the idea that, through hard work and aspiration, everybody can achieve what they want. For George and Lennie, this is the dream of owning their own land. It is so compelling that it draws Candy in and even Crooks, for a while. It is also potentially more than a dream, as George says he knows a place they could buy and Candy offers to put in more than half the money.

George and Lennie's dream is so compelling it influences Candy and Crooks

> **Key quotations**
>
> They fell into a silence. They looked at one another, amazed. This thing they had never really believed in was coming true. George said reverently, "Jesus Christ! I bet we could swing her." His eyes were full of wonder. "I bet we could swing her," he repeated softly. *(Chapter 3)*

While the plans of George, Lennie and Candy look to be achievable, those of Curley's wife are simply self-deluding. She goes on believing the stale chat-up lines she has received from men who told her they could get her "in pitchers". She dwells on her lost opportunities but is unable to get any closer to making her dream happen.

For George, Lennie and Candy their dream is snatched away just as it appears to come within reach. It seems as though the characters in the book are doomed to be disappointed and their dreams remain, as Crooks puts it, forever "in their heads" *(Chapter 4)* and therefore forever unfulfilled.

Activity 9

The reciting of the dream can be compared with a fairy tale, a myth and a religious ritual in the way it is told and the effect it has on its listeners. Look at the way Steinbeck has woven the idea of the dream into the text.

- The first telling of the story towards the end of Chapter 1 from **"Guys like us, that work on ranches..."** to **"...rain comin' down on the roof"**.

- Candy overhears the story in Chapter 3 from **"George, how long's it gonna be..."** to **"I bet we could swing her..."**.

- Lennie and Candy's conversation near the end of Chapter 4 from **'Lennie leaned towards the old swamper...'** to **'They swung their heads towards the door'**.

- Candy's repetition of certain details close to the end of Chapter 5 from **"I could of hoed in the garden..."** to **"an' us jus' settin' there"**.

- George's final telling near the close of the narrative in Chapter 6 from **"We gonna get a little place..."** to **"... like you can almost see the place"**.

Make notes on the following:

a) **Phrases** – which phrases are used each time the story is told?

b) **Storytelling** – why does Lennie insist on George telling the story although he seems to know it off by heart?

c) **Details** – what extra details are included at different tellings?

d) **Importance** – why is the dream important to George, Lennie and Candy?

e) **Crooks** – what does the dream represent, briefly, to Crooks?

The role of women

There is only one main female character in the novella and she has no name of her own. Curley's wife is married to a ranch worker but does not seem at all suited to life on a ranch. She is referred to as "a tramp", "a tart", "jail bait" in Chapter 2 and "a looloo" in Chapter 3 (presumably based on her dress and make-up and her flirtatious manner) even though she does not actually have much male company. Her marriage to Curley is clearly an unhappy and unequal one. Neither is interested in the other as a human being and, after only two weeks, Curley is off visiting the brothel on a Saturday night.

Curley is also absurdly jealous. Even if he doesn't want to spend time with his wife, he regards her as a possession that is not to be looked at by others.

Curley's wife is treated with mistrust by most of the men on the ranch

Activity 10

Work in groups of four to prepare for a class debate based on the following statements:

a) Curley's wife is a mean woman who throws herself at men and deserves all she gets.

b) In spite of her bad behaviour and lack of education we still feel sorry for Curley's wife.

As a group, choose to argue in support of one of the statements. Prepare your arguments and discuss your ideas within your group before taking part in the debate as a class. Remember to back up your points with evidence and quotations from the book.

The only other women whom Steinbeck refers to in the narrative are:

● Lennie's Aunt Clara, a motherly person who cared for Lennie and asked George to look after him before she died

● 'Old Susy' who runs a brothel in the nearby town.

With the men travelling on the road most of the time there is little chance for them to meet the kind of woman who would want to be married and look after a home. In this world, Steinbeck suggests, there is only room for mothers or prostitutes. George tells Lennie as much in Chapter 3: "You give me a good whore house every time" [...] "A guy can go in an' get drunk and get ever'thing outta his system all at once, an' no messes. And he knows how much it's gonna set him back." This reflects the men's view of women as sex objects and the reason they avoid women like Curley's wife. Steinbeck has been criticized for presenting women in this way, but he is portraying them as seen by the characters, not necessarily by himself.

Writing about themes

Upgrade

The way you approach themes in your assessment will depend on the question you have been asked. You may well be asked to focus on one particular theme, such as nature, loneliness or the importance of dreams. In this case you need to show how the author brings out these themes in the novella through different characters and events.

Even if the question does not specifically ask you about themes, you should still show that you have understood them. For example, if you are writing about the character of Candy, you can show how Steinbeck tackles the themes of loneliness, prejudice, violence and dreams through the way Candy behaves and what he says.

You should also look at how ideas develop as the book progresses. For example, does violence become more significant at the end of the book than it is at the beginning? Do certain events in the story make the theme more dominant or more complex? For example, does the scene in the harness room bring the theme of racial prejudice to the foreground? How is prejudice shown at different times in the story by and towards different characters?

Exam skills

Understanding the question

Look at the number of marks awarded for each section of the question. Then divide the time you have available to write the answer in proportion to the marks. For example, if you have 45 minutes to answer a two-part question where part a) is worth 7 marks and part b) is worth 20 marks, it is clear you should spend no more than ten minutes on part a) and 30 minutes on part b), allowing five minutes for planning. If the two parts are worth 10 marks each, you should aim to spend 20 minutes on each part.

Try to approach the question in a methodical way. Start by identifying what the question is actually asking you to do. You could do this by underlining the key words and phrases in the question and writing in what they mean. Examiners use certain words and phrases quite often. Learn what they mean and you will know what you need to write about.

'**Explore**' means look at all the different aspects of something. For example, 'Explore how the author makes Lennie a sympathetic character' means you need to look at his character as shown with George; as it is seen by Crooks and by Slim; as it is shown to the reader when he is on his own at the end of the book. Then you could look at how he is treated by Curley and by Curley's wife and his relationship with animals. Finally you might consider his role as the 'wise fool' and his belief in the dream farm.

'**How does the author...**' or '**show how...**' means explain the techniques the author uses to gain an effect. For example, 'How does Steinbeck make this episode tense?' means you need to look at how he builds up suspense or tension in the way he structures the scene; how he uses language such as verbs and descriptions to make the reader feel excitement or fear; how he uses the speech and actions of various characters to convey their emotions.

'**Present**' and '**portray**' are similar words for looking at a character and they prompt you to consider not only what the character is like, but also what devices the author uses to show this. For example, 'How is Curley presented/portrayed?' means you need to think about how he is described; what the author makes him say and do, and why; how the author reveals the reactions of other characters and how Steinbeck shows the character as important to the story as a whole. It is also very important to consider the character's voice and how Steinbeck uses linguistic devices to help develop a sense of his character.

'In what ways...' means look at different sides of something. For example, 'In what ways is the friendship between George and Lennie important?' means that you need to look at more than just the way they stick together. You need to consider how this contrasts with the other itinerant workers; the way in which George is both caring towards and irritated by Lennie; the significance of their shared belief in the dream farm; how they draw people to them (and make other people suspicious); and finally the way in which George kills Lennie out of love, despite knowing that Lennie is necessary to make his own dream a reality.

'How far...' means the examiner wants you to evaluate the extent of something. For example, 'How far is the dream of George and Lennie's farm important...?' means that you need to analyse how significant the dream is within the novella; what it means to the characters who share it; how it is related to the wider context of the American Dream; what it symbolizes and the impact of its destruction.

'What role...' prompts you to think about the importance of a character and the character's function in the novella. For example, 'What role does Candy play?' is asking you to think about why Steinbeck chose to include him in the novella. He is a weak character who reveals the harshness of a society which doesn't care for the old and infirm; his gossipy nature allows the reader to learn about the other characters; he enables George and Lennie to come within close reach of achieving their dream; and he adds to the tragedy of the ending, where he is shown to be cruelly let down by Lennie's actions.

'Explain' or **'comment on'** invites you to give your response to something in as much detail as you can. For example, 'Explain the importance of loneliness in the novella' means you should write about the way in which this is a feature of several of the characters' lives; that it leads to them spending their money as a means of seeking escape; that it is key to the tragedy because it leads Curley's wife to seek out Lennie; that it is connected, in some ways, to prejudice; and that ultimately it shows George's courage in killing Lennie.

Tips for assessment

Upgrade

To reach the higher marks you need to show that you have thought about the book for yourself and can give your own opinions about what the author is saying and how he is saying it, supporting your ideas with relevant references and quotations.

Look at the question below. The key words and phrases have been highlighted and explained.

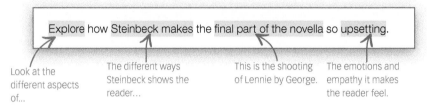

Explore how Steinbeck makes the final part of the novella so upsetting.

Look at the different aspects of...

The different ways Steinbeck shows the reader...

This is the shooting of Lennie by George.

The emotions and empathy it makes the reader feel.

You are being asked to do a number of things in this question. You need to look at the methods Steinbeck uses to:

- bring out the relationship between George and Lennie
- reveal George's feelings to the reader
- show Lennie's lack of understanding about the situation
- make the reader aware of the necessity of George's actions
- show the reactions of the other men.

Activity 1

Write out the following question.

Explore the importance of dreams within the novella as a whole.

a) Highlight or underline the key words in the question and then describe what you are being asked to do.

b) Make a bullet-point list of things you need to do to answer the question.

Planning your answer

It is worth taking five minutes to plan your answer before you start to write it. There are various ways in which you can do this.

Lists

You can list points that you want to make, making sure that each point focuses on the question. You can do this by arranging your list in two columns. An example plan is included on the opposite page in response to the question below:

Explore how Steinbeck makes the final part of the novella so upsetting.

Technique (how)	Effects (why upsetting)
1. Introduction – the relationship between George and Lennie and how it started	1. Shows George's role as carer, although at the end he feels he has to kill Lennie
2. Situational irony that results from George's earlier comments about wanting to be free of Lennie	2. At the end George learns a painful lesson in just how lonely he will be without Lennie
3. The way Steinbeck shows that shooting Lennie will end George's dream	3. The reader realizes how important Lennie is for George's happiness
4. Dramatic irony – the way that Lennie is unaware of the consequences of his actions	4. Steinbeck shows how helpless Lennie is, which makes the ending more tragic
5. Dialogue – the manner in which George prepares Lennie so he will die happy	5. Emotional because it shows an act of love in the face of hopelessness
6. Verbs/adjectives – how Steinbeck shows George's struggle to shoot his friend	6. Shows how terrible the situation is for George and allows the reader to sympathize with him
7. Characterization – Steinbeck makes the reader certain, through his characterization of Curley, that it will be worse for Lennie to be caught	7. Highlights the difficulty of the situation for George and Lennie; they are victims of a harsh society
8. Foreshadowing – Steinbeck makes the ending seem inevitable through earlier events in the novella	8. The reader knows there is no escape for either character
9. Dialogue – the different reactions of Slim and Carlson	9. Slim understands friendship, others do not. Perhaps there is some hope here, or perhaps it suggests that society is unlikely to learn from the tragic events in the story

 Activity 2

1. Create a two-column plan for each of the following questions:

   a) How does Steinbeck create a sense of insecurity in *Of Mice and Men*?

   b) How important do you consider the character of Crooks to be in the novella?

   c) How does Steinbeck show the negative effects of prejudice in the novella?

2. In groups of two or three, compare the plans you have created. Exchange ideas and add to your plans as necessary. Add stars next to what you consider to be the most important points in each plan. Be prepared to discuss your ideas with the class.

Spider diagrams

You could also use a spider diagram to plan your points, like the one below, which presents a plan for the question:

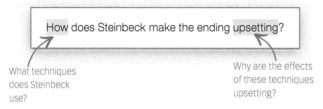

How does Steinbeck make the ending upsetting?

What techniques does Steinbeck use?

Why are the effects of these techniques upsetting?

Again, you need to ensure that your plan remains focused on the key words of the question, as highlighted above.

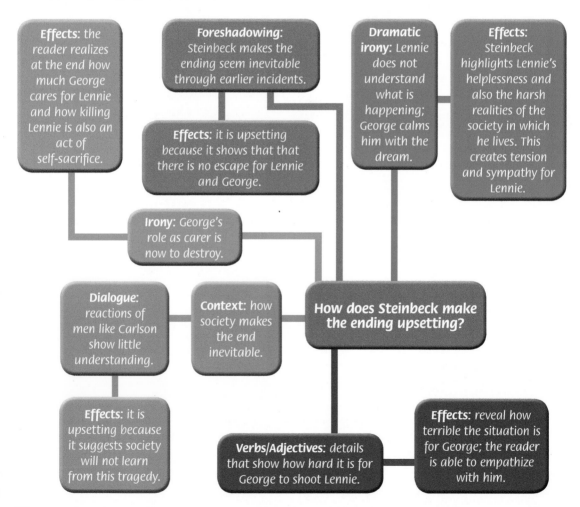

Effects: the reader realizes at the end how much George cares for Lennie and how killing Lennie is also an act of self-sacrifice.

Foreshadowing: Steinbeck makes the ending seem inevitable through earlier incidents.

Dramatic irony: Lennie does not understand what is happening; George calms him with the dream.

Effects: Steinbeck highlights Lennie's helplessness and also the harsh realities of the society in which he lives. This creates tension and sympathy for Lennie.

Effects: it is upsetting because it shows that that there is no escape for Lennie and George.

Irony: George's role as carer is now to destroy.

Dialogue: reactions of men like Carlson show little understanding.

Context: how society makes the end inevitable.

How does Steinbeck make the ending upsetting?

Effects: it is upsetting because it suggests society will not learn from this tragedy.

Verbs/Adjectives: details that show how hard it is for George to shoot Lennie.

Effects: reveal how terrible the situation is for George; the reader is able to empathize with him.

Activity 3

Use a spider diagram to plan an answer to each of the following questions:

a) In what ways does Steinbeck show the uses and abuses of power in *Of Mice and Men*?

b) Look at the passage from the start of the book up to Lennie's question, **"Where we going', George?"** (about four pages into the book). How well does this set the scene for everything that happens afterwards?

Writing your answer

Once you have a plan, you will have a clear idea of what you need to write to answer the question effectively. It might be helpful to prioritize your points by highlighting the ones you would like to cover first. You could do this by numbering your points in order of importance. You should also try to have an idea in mind of how you intend to finish your answer.

When you write, it is important that you make correct use of spelling, punctuation and grammar.

Tips for assessment

- Plan your time carefully in the exam. Don't spend too long on your plan or you will run out of time to complete your answer.

- Don't cross out your plan, because if you do run out of time you may be given credit for it.

Using (PEE) Point, Evidence, Explanation

Examiners want to see that you can support your ideas with evidence and that you are able to understand the various levels of meaning within the text. For example, you might make the point:

> George cannot bear the thought of shooting Lennie, whom he has always protected.

Your evidence for this might be:

> Steinbeck shows this when George picks up the gun and his hand shakes so much he has to put it down again.

Your explanation might be:

> George knows that Lennie will be better off dying quickly and painlessly but the reality of doing this seems beyond him and he carries on telling the familiar story, putting off the deed until the last possible moment. Steinbeck builds tension in this scene by juxtaposing the sounds of the approaching lynch mob with George's repetition of the familiar tale.

Tips for assessment

Upgrade

While PEE is a helpful reminder of what you need to build into your writing, you do not need to follow this pattern for every single point you make. It is useful for the important points, but you should avoid getting bogged down with unnecessary repetition. To reach the higher marks, you need to control your argument and try to keep your answer flowing.

Using quotations

Examiners will want to see that you can use quotations to support your points. When you make a point, ask yourself: 'How do I know this?' Usually it will be because of something the author has written – this is the quotation you need.

For example, you might make the point:

> Slim is well respected by everyone on the ranch and they all look up to him.

How do you know this? Well, there might be a number of quotations you could choose, but here is one:

> 'Candy looked helplessly at him, for Slim's opinions were law.' (Chapter 3)

By using this quotation you will show that you:

- can select relevant quotations to support your answer
- have understood that Slim is respected and people accept his judgements
- have understood that this relates to an important trait of his character.

To show skills of a higher level, try to use **embedded quotations**. These short quotations (usually of words or phrases) are easy to build into the flow of your own writing and you can also analyse them closely. For example: 'Steinbeck compares Slim to 'royalty' and a 'temple dancer' (Chapter 2), which immediately sets him apart from the other men.' Embedded quotations appear within the main text of your writing and they are marked using quotation marks in the usual way.

> **embedded quotations** short quotations of words or phrases that you can build into the flow of your writing

Achieving the best marks

Upgrade

To achieve high marks, you will need to do the following:

- show an assured or perceptive understanding of the book's themes and ideas
- show a pertinent or convincing response to the text
- select evidence that is relevant, detailed and sustained
- make references to context that are pertinent, convincing and supported by relevant textual reference
- use sentences that are sophisticated and varied; show precise control of expression and meaning; use a full range of punctuation and spelling that is consistently accurate.

In practice this means that you need to show that you have understood the book on more than one level. On the surface it is a story about two ranch hands travelling in order to find work and how one of them commits an unintentional murder and is killed by his friend. On an underlying level it is a criticism of the author's society and the way in which society fails to help the struggling and the weak. On a deeper level still it is a novella about the human condition, the fall of man and the loss of paradise.

In addition to the meaning of the novella, you need to show an awareness and understanding of the author's techniques. You need to show that you understand the narrative structure, such as why Steinbeck chooses to use a third-person viewpoint. You will also need to show that you have considered the importance of significant features of the text such as the use of dialogue and how Steinbeck uses this to present characters and reveal relationships. For every technique you identify, you need to show how and why Steinbeck uses it and the effect it has on the reader.

Sample questions

1

> ### *Of Mice and Men*
>
> Answer part (a) and **either** part (b) **or** part (c).
>
> **(a)** *Read the extract from eight pages into Chapter 2, from 'The old man came slowly into the room' to "He's a nice fella" [...] "You got to take him right".*
>
> What impressions do you get of Candy here? Give reasons for what you say and remember to support your answer with quotations from the extract.
>
> ### Either
> **(b)** What do you think about Curley?
>
> Think about:
> * his relationship with other characters
> * the way he speaks and behaves
> * anything else you think important.
>
> ### Or
> **(c)** Dreams are an important theme in *Of Mice and Men*. Write about some of the ways in which dreams are shown in different parts of the novella.
>
> Think about:
> * characters who have dreams
> * what life is like for those characters
> * anything else you think important.

2

> ### *Of Mice and Men*
>
> Answer part (a) and **either** part (b) **or** part (c).
>
> **(a)** *Read the extract from eight pages into Chapter 2, from 'The old man came slowly into the room' to "He's a nice fella" [...] "You got to take him right".*
>
> With close reference to the extract, show how John Steinbeck presents Candy's character here.
>
> ### Either
> **(b)** How does Steinbeck's presentation of Curley throughout the text affect your feelings towards him?
>
> ### Or
> **(c)** Dreams are the most important thing in the story. How far would you agree with this statement?

3

Of Mice and Men

Either (a)
Explain the importance of Slim in the novella.

In your answer you **must** consider:
- the relationship between Slim and the other people on the ranch
- the way Slim behaves to George and Lennie
- the differences between Slim and the other men.

You may include other ideas of your own.

Use **evidence** to support your answer.

Or (b)
Why is prejudice so important in the novella?

In your answer you **must** consider:
- the ways in which prejudice is shown against others
- people who are treated with prejudice
- how they try to cope with their situation.

You may include other ideas of your own.

Use **evidence** to support your answer.

4

Of Mice and Men

Either (a)
Explain the importance of Slim in the novella.

You **must** consider the context of the novella.

Use **evidence** to support your answer.

Or (b)
Explore how prejudice affects individual characters in the novella.

You **must** consider the context of the novella.

Use **evidence** to support your answer.

5

Of Mice and Men

Either (a)
Look at the extract close to the end of Chapter 6 from 'Lennie said, "I thought you was mad at me, George"' to the end of the book.

What do you think makes this such a powerful ending to the novella?

You should consider:
- how George acts and feels
- how the other men behave
- the words and phrases Steinbeck uses.

Or (b)
What are your feelings about Lennie and the way he is treated in the book?

Remember to support your ideas with details from the novella.

6

Of Mice and Men

Either (a)
Look at the extract close to the end of Chapter 6, from 'Lennie said, "I thought you was mad at me, George"' to the end of the book.

How does Steinbeck's writing make this such a powerful and moving ending to the novella?

Or (b)
How much sympathy with Lennie does Steinbeck make you feel throughout the novella?

Remember to support your ideas with details from the book.

7

Of Mice and Men

Read the passage and then answer the questions that follow.

Look at the extract that begins four pages from the start of Chapter 5, from "If George sees me talkin' to you he'll give me hell" to '... her little finger stuck out grandly from the rest'.

(a) How does Steinbeck use details in the passage to show what Curley's wife is like?

(b) How is Curley's wife treated by the other characters in the whole novella and what does this show you about the society she lived in?

You should think about:
- what she does and what happens to her
- the attitudes of the other people on the ranch towards Curley's wife.

8

Of Mice and Men

Read the passage and then answer the questions that follow.

Look at the extract that begins four pages from the start of Chapter 5, from "If George sees me talkin' to you he'll give me hell" to '... her little finger stuck out grandly from the rest'.

(a) How do the details in this passage add to your understanding of Curley's wife?

(b) How does Steinbeck use the character of Curley's wife in the novella as a whole to convey ideas about America in the 1930s?

Sample answers

Sample answer 1

Below is a sample answer from a student, together with examiner comments, to the following general question on the novella:

> What part does the theme of violence and anger play in the novella?
> In your answer you should consider:
>
> - how violence is used by different characters
> - why these characters use violence
> - what effect it has on others.

There is a lot of violence in this book. Curley uses violence because he is angry. He is the most violent character because he does it deliberately. He acts violently towards Lennie and George the first time he meets them. He was a boxing champion and he likes to pick on people who are bigger than him. He later picks a fight with Lennie because he is smiling and Curley thinks he is laughing at him, although Lennie is actually smiling because he is thinking of the dream farm and his rabbits. Curley batters Lennie and Lennie tries to move away as George has told him to, but Curley just keeps punching him until George tells Lennie to "get him". Then Lennie uses violence by crushing Curley's hand and then Lennie gets upset in case George won't let him tend the rabbits. This leads to Curley wanting to kill Lennie after he kills Curley's wife and he leads a lynch mob after Lennie. This is similar to what happened in Weed, but this time Lennie has done something much worse.

Lennie uses violence because he likes to pet soft things but then he gets scared when they try to get free and he tries to stop them. He doesn't realize how strong he is so they get hurt or killed. This is what happened to the mice at the beginning of the book. It is also what happens to his puppy and Curley's wife. Lennie doesn't mean to be violent and he knows when he has done "a bad thing" and that George will be mad at him. He is like a child in a man's body and children often don't understand about being gentle with things.

Another person who is violent is Carlson and he has his own pistol which is a Luger. He shows violence when he kills Candy's dog just because it is old and smelly. He does not think about

Examiner comments:

Point could be developed, but makes distinction about intentions.

Uses an example for evidence but without explanation.

A re-telling of the fight without explaining its significance.

Relevant examples but needs to consider Steinbeck's choices.

Understanding of Lennie's motives.

Good examples but needs following up.

Some attempt to explain why Lennie is violent, which shows thought.

Good use of embedded quotation but without explanation. For example, the student could emphasize the selfish motivations behind the killing of Candy's dog.

Well-chosen quotation but not evaluated.

Valid personal comment that shows insight.

Perceptive point about George's use of violence and motives.

Good understanding but this point could be developed even further.

Recital of angry characters and brief motives but no consideration of the part this plays in the novella.

Again some attempt at explaining motive but doesn't weigh up the part that this plays in the novella.

Weak ending repeats the question rather than making a fresh point.

how much it means to Candy. He won't even wait for the next day, because he says "We can't sleep with him stinkin' around in here." Carlson uses violence to get rid of animals who are no longer useful and people who have done something criminal, like when he goes after Lennie with Curley at the end of the book but he has no idea how bad it was for George to have to shoot Lennie because he says to Curley "Now what the hell ya suppose is eatin' them two guys?" I think Carlson just sees violence as part of his way of life as he has no sympathy with people like Candy or Lennie who were social misfits in those days.

George uses violence when he kills Lennie but unlike the others in the book he does it out of love because he knows a lynch mob is after Lennie and he wants him to die peacefully. He tells Lennie the story about the dream farm and then shoots him painlessly. This is the same way Carlson killed Candy's dog but it is different for George as he knows it is the end of his dreams and he does it for good reasons.

People in the book are often angry. Lennie worries that George will be mad at him – as he sometimes is, although George is always sorry afterwards. George gets angry at people who want to harm Lennie, like Curley. Candy gets angry with Curley's wife in Crooks's room because she is spoiling the chat they are having and then she verbally attacks Crooks and Candy himself. Curley's wife is angry with her husband and her mother because she thinks they spoiled her chances of becoming a film star. Sometimes this anger is because the characters have no power. Crooks gets angry because he is black and not allowed to mix with the other men which means he is very lonely.

So this is how the theme of violence and anger plays a big part.

Overall this candidate shows a good understanding of the question and has followed the bullet points. There is some attempt to support points with evidence and quotations are appropriate and embedded. However, this answer lacks a sense of deeper analysis and there is not much attempt to develop points in detail. This student could improve the answer by linking the points back to the question and by evaluating the meaning and importance of the quotations he/she has selected.

Sample answer 2

Below is a sample answer from a student, together with examiner comments, to the following passage-based question on the novella:

> *Read the extract from Chapter 2, from 'George stared at his solitaire lay' to "If I get in trouble".*
>
> How does Steinbeck bring out the nature of George and Lennie's friendship in this passage?

The friendship between George and Lennie is very unusual among itinerant workers at the time and Steinbeck has already shown how it causes comment from the boss of the ranch and, more unpleasantly, from his son, Curley. George is presented as almost a father to Lennie, in the way he warns him, "You try to keep away from him, will you?" because he knows that Curley will try to make himself look big by picking a fight with Lennie. George uses the word "try" because he knows it will be difficult if Curley is determined. Lennie is reliant on George telling him what to do and protecting him, and his childlike attitude is revealed by his appeal, "Don't let him sock me, George." This is reinforced during the fight when Curley is 'smashing' and 'slugging' at Lennie who cries out "Make 'um stop, George." Steinbeck gives him a touching faith in George's ability to look after him and we know, from the first chapter in the book, that Lennie would not survive without his friend.

Lennie's innocent assertion that "I never done nothing to him" shows his immature belief in fairness in a world where the Great Depression and the enforced migration of workers in search of jobs give little reason for such optimism. Steinbeck reinforces the impression that he would never be able to hold his own on a ranch without George. Steinbeck uses appropriate language to show Lennie's state of mind by using phrases like his 'eyes were frightened', showing how scared he is of Curley; 'Lennie mourned', which implies his grief at Curley's aggression; 'asked timidly', showing his worry at George's frown; 'eyes moved sadly', as he misunderstands that George is not threatening him. All of these phrases make us feel both sad and indignant on Lennie's behalf, and tell the reader that Lennie is incapable of dealing with someone like Curley. Most of Lennie's dialogue

Opening statement related to context but also to events in the narrative.

Establishes the nature of the relationship using appropriate quotations, which are evaluated.

Well chosen references to Steinbeck's use of language.

Contextual reference links to question directly.

Close language analysis shows sensitive awareness of Steinbeck's techniques.

Effective focus on Steinbeck's use of dislogue to create a distinct sense of character.

in this passage is appealing to George or asking him questions or repeating what George has said, all of which shows how dependent on George he is.

George tries to make Lennie understand how dangerous Curley could be, especially since he is the boss's son and could get them 'canned'. He frowns as he thinks what to do and Lennie immediately becomes anxious and asks if he's mad at him, showing how much Lennie dislikes being in George's bad books. Steinbeck wants the reader to realize this because it foreshadows Lennie's greatest fear which is that George will abandon him – a fear that Crooks plays on later and at the end of the book causes Lennie to hallucinate until George appears. It makes George's statement to Lennie at the end even more poignant when he says "I ain't mad. I never been mad, and I ain't now. That's a thing I want ya to know."

Good understanding of foreshadowing and appropriate references to other parts of the novella and their effect on the reader.

George wants Lennie to keep away from Curley, but tells him "...if the son-of-a-bitch socks you – let 'im have it." Lennie doesn't understand that George means him to retaliate and George reassures him by saying, "I'll tell you when." This part of the dialogue foreshadows the fight with Curley when Lennie fails to defend himself against Curley's punches until George orders him to. Steinbeck chooses to make Lennie misunderstand George in order to show both how innocent Lennie is and how inadequate he would be as an itinerant worker on his own. The author also wants us to understand how ill-fitted he is to cope with 'normal' life, which prepares us for the reasons that force George to kill him at the end; a desperate act of love which is all he can then do for Lennie.

Shows perceptive understanding of plot and structure, cause and effect, and the author's manipulation of the reader's response.

George then asks Lennie, in case of any real trouble with Curley, "Look, Lennie, if you get in any kind of trouble, you remember what I told you to do?" Lennie's response reveals his misunderstanding as he says, "If I get in any trouble, you ain't gonna let me tend the rabbits." This statement is related to the first chapter of the book and to the farm that George and Lennie dream of having where they will live off the fat of the land. This is the dream that keeps them going, more so because it is shared. The dream of being independent and owning a piece of land was common to many of those who had nothing but their (often unwanted) labour to offer. Steinbeck uses the rabbits as synecdoche for the whole dream, as Lennie regards them as his share of it. George tries to keep Lennie from getting into trouble

Comments show insight into the dream and its contribution to their relationship.

by using this threat, which is really for Lennie's protection. In spite of all his efforts Lennie does get into trouble with Curley, although not in the way he imagines. Steinbeck shows their relationship as being built around the ritual of the dream. Its repeated tellings have a mythical quality and contain the idea that it is unattainable. It is connected with Lennie to the extent of dying with him.

Thoughtful response to how Lennie's desire for soft things is fatal, George's paternal role and the profound nature of the dream.

The instructions George now gives Lennie are a repetition of the instructions he gave him in Chapter 1 and he makes Lennie repeat them yet again in the hope he will remember. Lennie has a tendency to forget things, which leads to him making the same mistakes and doing "bad things" again. Steinbeck uses this idea to create suspense within the novella as we expect Lennie to make a bad mistake and the way in which he sets up Lennie's reactions to Curley's wife makes it almost inevitable that she will figure in it. George knows this and his affection for Lennie makes him try to forestall the consequences, which, in the time the book was set, might well be a lynching – something they narrowly escaped before the novella opens. This part of their conversation not only reflects the previous incident in Weed that George relates to Slim, but foreshadows what happens after Lennie has killed Curley's wife.

Good understanding of plot, structure, reference to context and the effects of the author's techniques on the reader.

The relationship between George and Lennie has been likened to the two parts of a whole, with Lennie representing the child who must be put away as George becomes a 'whole' adult. Steinbeck has used ideas from the biblical story of Cain and Abel, the sons of Adam and Eve after their expulsion from Eden. Cain killed his brother and was then condemned to wander the Earth, and Steinbeck implies Cain's words to God, 'Am I my brother's keeper?' In the relationship between George and Lennie the answer must be simply 'Yes.'

Excellent conclusion that looks at biblical and psychological interpretations and the depth of the novella, and is not repetitious.

The candidate has shown a sophisticated understanding of the novella and of the author's intentions and techniques. Quotations are well chosen, embedded and evaluated, and the student also relates the passage briefly to context and to other parts of the novella in a thoughtful manner. The conclusion makes a new point, which lends impact to the argument.

Sample answer 3

Below is a sample answer from a student, together with examiner comments, to the following passage-based question:

> Read the passage which begins in Chapter 2, from 'Both men glanced up...' to "Bet she'd clear out for twenty bucks."
>
> How is Curley's wife treated by the other characters in the novella and what does this show you about the society she lived in?
>
> Write about:
> - what she does and what happens to her
> - the attitudes of other people on the ranch towards Curley's wife.

A fair point supported by evidence but not developed.

Makes a connection with earlier events in Weed but doesn't comment on structure or foreshadowing.

In the passage this is the first time we see Curley's wife. She is wearing a lot of make-up and red nail polish and mules with feathers. The word 'red' is repeated to tell us she is a flirt, as women like her were called 'a scarlet woman' in those times. She puts herself in a pose that shows off her figure and Lennie can't take his eyes off her. It was a red dress he tried to pet in Weed when he and George had to escape because the girl told everyone he tried to rape her.

Well chosen quotation but this point could be expanded to consider Steinbeck's choice of vocabulary.

It seems as if she has come in to check out the new men, although she says she is looking for Curley, which is just an excuse. It says 'She smiled archly and twitched her body' which tells us she wants to be noticed, but when Slim tells her he's seen Curley going into their house she hurries away, which tells us she is scared of Curley.

This point is valid but more could be said about the language and what it reveals about attitudes.

An attempt here to introduce context but this feels a little tacked-on.

She is treated as a threat by most of the men on the ranch and she is called "a tart", "a tramp" and "jail bait" and the men always try to get rid of her, as they know how jealous and possessive Curley is and how he could get them sacked. There were not many jobs available at this time because the Great Depression had made a lot of businesses go bankrupt and the dust bowl in the Midwest had driven people off their land to look for work. The men would not risk their jobs for Curley's wife and so she is lonely.

Curley does not look after his wife very well as he leaves her alone a lot and when he is there, he is always telling her about how he would fight people. He even leaves her alone on a Saturday night to go into town to a whorehouse. Women in those days were seen as tarts unless they stayed at home and baked cakes and looked after children, like Lennie's Aunt Clara. This is why Curley's wife dreams of being a film star, where she would be noticed and looked up to by everyone. "Coulda been in the movies, an' had nice clothes – all them nice clothes like they wear. An' I coulda sat in them big hotels…"

A well-made point supported by quotation but more could be said about what this reveals about her situation.

Her treatment by the ranch hands does not make her kinder to the people at the bottom of society. When she comes into Crooks's room while the men have all gone to town she behaves in a horrible way. She calls them "a nigger and a dum-dum and a lousy ol' sheep", which is very insulting and she knows they cannot do anything because she is the boss's wife who could get Candy the sack so he would have nowhere to go and Lennie too. She laughs at them because she knows she has the upper hand. Worst of all she could get Crooks lynched or executed because she is a white woman and she could accuse him of rape. He is not safe even in his own room because she just comes in and threatens him. She tells him "I could get you strung up on a tree so easy it ain't even funny."

Thoughtful discussion of her abuse of power. This could be expanded to say more about the idea of a ranch hierarchy.

She admires Lennie because he has 'busted' Curley and when she finds him in the barn the next day with his dead puppy she will not leave him alone. She tells him all about her dream of going into the movies and she keeps talking because he is the only one who listens to her. She shares his love of petting soft things and gets him to stroke her hair but when he is too rough she panics and tries to get away which makes Lennie panic and hold on until her neck is broken.

More could be said about what these events reveal about Curley's wife.

Some understanding shown of the situation but insufficient analysis.

She is referred to as trouble from the start of the book and at the end we see this is true because Lennie kills her and then George has to kill Lennie and everyone's dreams are destroyed.

The conclusion sums up the answer neatly although without much critical analysis.

The candidate has covered the points mentioned in the question and shown a good understanding of the events and characters. There is an attempt to relate it to context and good use of reference and quotation to support answers. However, this answer needs to show more awareness of the author's choices and the effects these choices have on the reader's understanding of Curley's wife and her situation.

Sample answer 4

Below is a sample answer from a student, together with examiner comments, to the following general question on the novella:

> How far do you consider dreams to be important to the characters in *Of Mice and Men*?

Good opening that establishes context economically and addresses the question directly.

The American Dream was built on the idea that with hard work and motivation anyone could achieve what they wanted, but Steinbeck's novella is set in the worst of times when the Great Depression is at its height and queues of jobless men wait in lines in hope of employment. George and Lennie are typical of the migrant workers at the time, travelling from place to place and working wherever hands are needed. Their dream, like many others, is to own a piece of land which they can farm themselves. The importance of this dream is shown in its repetition throughout the text. It is like a well-known story that Lennie never tires of hearing and, like the child he is inside, he can repeat parts of it word for word. This gives it the air of a fairy tale, which is appropriate since it never happens.

Good point about author's use of techniques and literary genre.

Steinbeck first includes the story of the dream farm in the first chapter, in the paradise setting of the pool. This is a very suitable background because this is George and Lennie's view of heaven. "Someday – we're gonna get the jack together and we're gonna have a little house and a couple of acres an' a cow and some pigs..." and Lennie interrupts with one of his favourite lines about living "off the fatta the lan' " and having rabbits. To Lennie the rabbits represent not only security but something he can look after and pet as much he wishes without getting into trouble. This association of the dream with Eden is reflected in the words of Crooks later on, when he says "Just like heaven. Ever'body wants a little piece of lan'. I read plenty of books out here. Nobody ever gets to heaven, and nobody gets no land."

Very good connection between dreams and heaven, which recognizes allegory and provides evidence.

The reader learns more about the dream farm later on, just after Candy's dog has been shot. George is telling Lennie about it and, in spite of his misery, old Candy is drawn into the dream as well. Steinbeck shows how powerful the dream is when Candy offers to put all his savings into the farm if he can share it, despite the fact that he has only just met George and Lennie. When they realize that this brings the dream to somewhere near reality, 'They all sat still, all bemused by the beauty of the thing…'. Their dream has become a plan. It is strong enough to appeal even to the cynical Crooks, who asks if he can come and work for his keep. Steinbeck allows the reader a very short time to imagine this idyllic set-up before Curley's wife reminds Crooks of his place in the hierarchy and he gives up any idea of joining them. Whether she intends it or not, she is the cause of the dream's ending. It is her death that makes it impossible as old Candy recognizes when he curses her body in a rage of fury and disappointment. The final repetition of the story is when Steinbeck shows George telling it to Lennie as he prepares to shoot him in the back of the head. The only way Lennie will find his bit of heaven is by dying and, in giving it to him, George sacrifices his own hopes, for he knows that, without Lennie, he will be just like the other men who spend their money on gambling, drinking and whoring to keep the loneliness at bay.

Curley's wife has her own dreams and, ironically, it is her insistence on sharing them with Lennie that leads to the destruction of the men's dream farm. She wants to be a film star and is pathetically ready to believe any man who tells her she is "a natural" and that he will put her "in pitchers" as she expresses it. Although she is a pretty girl, Steinbeck describes her as having a 'nasal voice' which would hardly go down well in an industry where talking pictures were now commonplace. After only two weeks, Curley deserts her for the whorehouse in town so it is hardly surprising that she dreams of being a star and the centre of attention. Her dreams are shown as being

Shows analysis of author's intentions and techniques regarding the power of the dream.

Well-explained points. There is an opportunity here to perhaps mention foreshadowing.

Perceptive analysis of Steinbeck's presentation of events.

Good point that recognizes Steinbeck's use of irony.

The absurdity of Curley's wife's dream is summed up here with effective reference to context.

There is some empathy for her dream and understanding of why she might hold onto it.

even more groundless than the dream farm and she is just another small town girl who yearns for fame.

Good conclusion that sums up the answer and moves it on to show the tragedy of lost dreams.

The dreams the characters are given by Steinbeck are ones shared by hundreds of men and women in America at the time when hardship and unemployment made people want to escape from real life. Steinbeck uses them to show how even a harsh life can be made bearable by hope and how bleak life looks without it.

Thise candidate has given a detailed, analytical and sophisticated answer that examines Steinbeck's presentation of dreams and links it to his use of allegory. It is well written and uses apt and well-placed quotations. It is clear this candidate has a solid grasp of the narrative and a perceptive understanding of the writer's intentions and techniques.

Glossary

accomplice a person who helps another to commit a crime

African-American Civil Rights Movement a political movement in the USA (1955–68) aimed at outlawing racial discrimination and giving voting and other rights to black citizens

bindle stiff a manual labourer who travelled from place to place to find work

bucking grain passing full bags of grain along a line of men and onto a cart

candy wagon a type of bus used for transporting people

cat house similar to whorehouse or brothel

cause and effect the way in which one event leads to another event

clause a part of a sentence that could form a sentence on its own

climax a turning point in the action of a novel; the moment where the action reaches its greatest intensity

confidant somebody who is entrusted with secrets

dialect a way of speaking that is characteristic of a particular group of people, such as those who live in the same geographical region

double negative using two negative forms together in a phrase or sentence, e.g. 'ain't going nowhere' instead of 'isn't going anywhere'

dramatic irony a literary technique by which the significance of a character's words or actions is clear to the audience or reader but not to the character

Eden the idyllic garden in which Adam and Eve lived before they were banished for disobeying God

elision leaving out one or more sounds from a word to make it easier to say

embedded quotations short quotations of words or phrases that you can build into the main flow of your writing

empathy understanding of another person's feelings

femme fatale a French phrase that is applied to any woman who has supposedly fatal powers of sexual attraction

figurative language language that uses 'figures of speech' such as metaphors, similes, personification, etc.

foreboding a prediction or omen that suggests something bad is going to happen

foreshadowing the use of events in a book that are later shown to have a connection with a more significant incident, e.g. the men who chase George and Lennie in Weed foreshadow the men who will hunt Lennie down at the end of the book

graybacks lice

Great Depression a period of severe economic depression, which affected people across the world in the 1930s

hyperbole exaggeration, used to express something strongly and not intended to be taken literally

idiom a phrase or expression which has a meaning that is specific to a certain dialect, e.g. 'don't you try to put nothing over', which means 'don't try to cheat me'

inciting incident an important event in the plot that triggers everything that happens later on

inevitability the way in which something becomes absolutely certain because of the circumstances leading up to it

ironic the way in which something is known to be the opposite of what is said

jack-pin a movable pin on a ship around which ropes are fastened

jail bait normally a girl under the age of consent; in *Of Mice and Men*, this term is used to refer to a woman who could tempt men into adultery

jerkline skinner the chief driver of a mule train. The mules would pull carts into which grain was loaded

Jim Crow laws a system of racial segregation laws enacted in the USA between 1876 and 1965

juxtaposition to place two images or ideas side-by-side to highlight the differences between them

liniment a rub that generates heat for soothing aching muscles and bones

lynching the illegal hanging of someone (usually from a tree) by a group or mob without a proper arrest or trial

mantra something repeated over as a chant or prayer

metaphor a comparison of one thing to another to make a description more vivid; a metaphor states that one thing is the other

monologue a long speech spoken by a character, usually reflecting on his/her internal thoughts and feelings

narrative perspective the viewpoint from which a story is told; e.g. this might be first person using 'I', 'me' and 'we' or third person using 'he', 'she' and 'they'

novella a prose text which is longer than a short story but shorter than a standard novel

onomatopoeia words that sound like the things they represent; e.g. 'crash', 'snap'

pathetic fallacy a figurative technique of using nature to reflect people's moods

personification a figurative technique of giving human characteristics to inanimate objects

phrase a group of words in a sentence that could not form a separate sentence

proletariat the common or working people

protagonists the central characters

public relief government aid for the poor

resolution how the climax or crisis in a narrative is worked out

rhetorical expressed in a way designed to persuade or impress the listener

rite a custom or practice performed as a means of showing commitment to and faith in a belief

scarlet woman a promiscuous woman or a prostitute

segregation the separation of white people and black people in many areas of life, such as accommodation, transport, education and public facilities

simile a comparison that shows it is comparing by using 'like' or 'as'

situational irony created when there is a difference between what is expected to happen and what actually happens

slug a single measure of spirits

smallholding a property smaller than a normal farm

stable buck a racist term for a black stable lad or groom

stock market a virtual market in which company shares are traded across the world

swamper a cleaner

understatement a limited or restrained manner of expressing yourself that leaves a lot unsaid, but implies more than is said

Wall Street Crash a devastating stock market crash in 1929 which signalled the beginning of the Great Depression

Women's Liberation Movement a broadly based political movement (1965–present) dedicated to giving women equal rights with men under the law, in the workplace and in society

work agencies places that matched workers to employers, similar to our job centres. They would advance fares to the workers they placed and would then claim these, and their commission, back from their wages

Great Clarendon Street, Oxford OX2 6DP

Oxford University Press is a department of the University of Oxford.
It furthers the University's objective of excellence in research,
scholarship, and education by publishing worldwide in

Oxford   New York

Auckland   Cape Town   Dar es Salaam   Hong Kong   Karachi
Kuala Lumpur   Madrid   Melbourne   Mexico City   Nairobi
New Delhi   Shanghai   Taipei   Toronto

With offices in

Argentina   Austria   Brazil   Chile   Czech Republic   France   Greece
Guatemala   Hungary   Italy   Japan   Poland   Portugal   Singapore
South Korea   Switzerland   Thailand   Turkey   Ukraine   Vietnam

Oxford is a registered trade mark of Oxford University Press
in the UK and in certain other countries

British Library Cataloguing in Publication Data

Data available

ISBN 978-0-19-839042-8
Kindle edition ISBN 978-0-19-836895-3

10 9 8 7 6

Printed by CPI Group (UK) Ltd, Croydon CR0 4YY

Acknowledgements
The publisher and author are grateful for permission to reprint the following copyright material:

Extracts from *Of Mice and Men* by John Steinbeck (Penguin, 2006), copyright © John Steinbeck 1937,
1965, reprinted by permission of Penguin Books Ltd

Extract from the speech given by Anders Osterling when awarding John Steinbeck with the Nobel
Prize for Literature, 1962, copyright © The Nobel Foundation, reprinted with their permission.

Cover: Dorothea Lange/Library of Congress; **p6:** Moviestore Collection Ltd/Alamy; **p9:** AF archive/
Alamy; **p11:** Moviestore Collection Ltd/Alamy; **p13:** AF archive/Alamy; **p16:** Herbert Zettl/Corbis;
p20: Pictorial Press Ltd/Alamy; **p21:** Everett Collection Historical/Alamy; **p22:** Everett Collection
Historical/Alamy; **p24:** Moviestore Collection Ltd/Alamy; **p25:** Everett Collection Historical/Alamy;
p26: Andrew Darrington/Alamy; **p30:** AF archive/Alamy; **p31:** AF archive/Alamy; **p35:** Moviestore
Collection Ltd/Alamy; **p37:** Moviestore Collection Ltd/Alamy; **p43:** Bettmann/CORBIS; **p50:** Arthur
Rothstein/CORBIS; **p52:** KingWu/Getty; **p53:** Robert Shantz/Alamy; **p55:** kreego/Shutterstock;
p58: Stefano Bianchetti/Corbis; **p61:** Yeko Photo Studio/Shutterstock; **p62:** Time & Life Pictures/
Getty Images; **p65:** kuppa/Shutterstock; **p67:** Moviestore Collection Ltd/Alamy; **p68:** artjazz/
Shutterstock; **p70:** Ronald Grant Archive